YELLOW WORKOUT BOOK: RESISTANCE BAND STRENGTH TRAINING FOR SENIORS

AT-HOME AND ON-THE-GO EXERCISES TO IMPROVE
STRENGTH AND HEALTHY AGING

ROBERT L. STONEBRIDGE

Yellow
Workout Book

CONTENTS

MEDICAL ADVICE DISCLAIMER

DISCLAIMER: THIS BOOK DOES NOT PROVIDE MEDICAL ADVICE

The contents contained within this book are not to be used as a substitute for professional medical diagnosis, advice, or treatment. The information found in this book is for informational purposes only, and should you have any questions regarding medical conditions and/or treatment, this should be taken up with a qualified healthcare provider. The same is true when you wish to experiment with new healthcare regimens. Professional medical guidance and advice should never be delayed or disregarded as a result of anything that was learned in this book.

INTRODUCTION

 Aging is an extraordinary process where you become the person you always should have been.

— DAVID BOWIE

With age comes a wide range of changes not only to the human body, but also to the mind. Oftentimes the mental side of your health is still very much intact, while your physical performance takes the biggest blow. This is evident in research that displays the severity of the uncontrollable decrease of one's muscle power, tissue, and functionality. This occurrence is called sarcopenia, and is believed to take place every decade after age 30. About 3–8% of one's muscle tissue is lost during this time and that percentage is believed to increase even more as you surpass your 60s (Volpi et al., 2004). It's important to note that this process (sarcopenia) is completely involuntary, and many of the disabilities in the elderly can be attributed to this.

Sarcopenia works by basically elevating your susceptibility to injury and falling, which may then lead to disability or physical incapacitation. Aside from these already scary consequences, the loss of muscle mass can additionally bring about modifications of your body composition, as well as cause a spike in fat mass.

These modifications can further lead to more severe conditions like osteoporosis, heart disease, obesity, insulin resistance, lowered bone density, stiffness in the joints, or type 2 diabetes. It can also cause the phenomenon known as kyphosis, also known as roundback or hunchback. This is an abnormality of the spine causing excessive curvature of the upper back. Causing pain and stiffness.

WHAT CAUSES SARCOPENIA?

Unfortunately, there are no set causes for this detrimental occurrence; however, there are various hypotheses available. The modifications that take place in your body composition after a certain age is believed to result in a decrease in the amount of cells in your muscles, as well as the proportions of sarcoplasmic reticulum—which is responsible for the administration of calcium, vital to how effectively muscles relax and contract.

In addition to this, it also reduces muscle reaction time and force. The muscle cells become enveloped by fat build-up due to the disorderly spacing of the contractile system of the muscle fiber, which causes the muscle's plasma membrane to be less reactive. This is one possible explanation for the occurrence of sarcopenia; however, researchers believe that there are a range of elements that influence it. Despite the various suspected causes, it's believed that physical activity, adequate nutrition, and endocrine functions can be improved with the assistance of medication and physical activity (Volpi et al., 2004).

INTRODUCING PHYSICAL ACTIVITY

It goes without saying that you may be doubting your ability to start regular physical activity, especially if your muscle tissue already seems to be taking a dip. There is light at the end of the tunnel, however, as I will be explaining why resistance bands will soon be your new best friend. For those who don't know what a resistance band is, it's a rubber band that is stretched using certain parts of the body that is helpful to get those muscles working.

This exercise regimen is increasing in popularity, and the reason for this is its astounding versatility and effectiveness. Regardless of the fitness level, band resistance has some amazing effects on your body, and seniors especially can benefit from it. Resistance bands are a great way to build and strengthen muscles without having to do any strenuous weight lifting.

What Are the Benefits?

Nursing homes introduced the use of resistance bands as a means to help the elderly build physical sturdiness. More and more people realized just how beneficial these bands were and started using them in their general workout routines. Some of the benefits that come with resistance band exercise are:

- **Mobility.** Unlike excruciatingly heavy weights or complex training machines, the resistance band is compact and fits into most bags, so you're not restricted to working out in one area.
- **Affordability.** Admittedly, exercise equipment can be on the pricey side; however, the cost of a set of quality resistance bands can range between $20–$80. Resistance band allows you to do strength training without needing to buy weights or expensive equipment.
- **Versatility.** The extremity of the resistance can be adjusted by lengthening and shortening the band. This means the intensity of the workout is adjustable to your preference. You can practice a variety of exercises with just one band, so it provides you with lots of versatility.

These bands are a straightforward way to gently strengthen your muscles as well as increase your flexibility, and you can do so at your own pace. Moreover, resistance band exercise helps support improved mobility on both macro and micro levels. My experience as a rehab and strength-training instructor has provided me with a wealth of knowledge in helping seniors improve their quality of life for many decades, and I'm an advocate for the immense difference it makes in their lives. I've personally seen people who once found difficulty moving show substantial improvement with simple tasks and activities.

No matter where you're currently finding yourself in terms of your fitness, there's never a reason for you to give up on yourself. Rather than simply taking my word for it, try out resistance band training and experience the positive changes for yourself.

The ultimate goal is to be able is to be able to play with your grandchildren or socialize with your neighbors, to have stamina, to improve your performance in a sporting event like pickleball or squash, to feel independent and empowered, to have more autonomy, more energy, more mental clarity, and peace—so that you may enjoy the years ahead with inspiration, encouragement, and lightness.

To help yourself stay focused and on track, make a list of the fitness goals you'd like to achieve and the reasons why you're interested in band strength training. Whenever you're feeling like you can't continue or like it's too hard, read it again, as this will help keep you motivated and remind you why you're doing what you're doing.

Now, without further ado, join me on your journey to achieve better mobility and improved overall health.

1

BENEFITS OF STRENGTH TRAINING

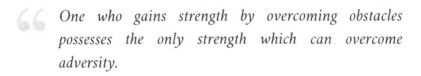 *One who gains strength by overcoming obstacles possesses the only strength which can overcome adversity.*

— ALBERT SCHWEITZER

As much as we would like to believe that our old age will be seamless or that we are or are going to be that one-in-a-million case where our physical health won't suffer by the age of 60, the truth is that without taking the necessary steps, this outcome is inevitable. Flexibility, muscle strength, and the general ability to do certain things takes a considerable decline by this age, and this can be quite taxing on your mental well-being as well. You're constantly annoyed and frustrated because you simply can't do the things you once could, and have no idea where to go from there.

Performing consistent and frequent strength training offers us the ability to regain control over our mobility. This, coupled with resistance and balance exercises, can make major improvements to joint lubrication and bone density, and is believed to even combat muscle loss. The reason why strength training is so great for firmer and denser bones is because of the pushing and pulling of the bones, which stimulates activity from the *osteoblasts*, also referred to as "bone-forming cells".

Strength training isn't only about getting physically stronger and growing muscles, as it can also help increase your bone density. You shouldn't only prioritize resistance strength training to see the muscle growth, but you must do it for the benefits you experience internally that you may not physically see. Having stronger bones will decrease your risk of breaking bones or suffering with osteoporosis. The United States is believed to have approximately 2 million men and an astounding 8 million women ailing with this disease (Harvard Health, 2021).

We often undermine the seriousness of osteoporosis, because we don't know just how significantly this disease can impact our lives until it's too late. It not only increases your chances of breaking bones easier; it also reduces your chances of full recovery after injury. That said, bone mass isn't only reduced as a result of aging. There are various other factors that increase the likelihood of significant loss of bone mass, such as lack of physical activity and poor diet.

This reality may scare you as you realize that you too could succumb to this in your upcoming years; however, research suggests that strength training has the potential to delay bone loss, as well as help develop bone, meaning there's hope after all (Harvard Health, 2021).

Strength training centered around balance and force is highly beneficial, as it improves your physical capabilities and improves your self-esteem and mood. As you increase your muscle mass through strength training, you burn more fat as opposed to muscle. This is essential if, in addition to your other goals, you're also hoping to lose weight. The reason behind fat being burned faster is that your metabolic rate is elevated, which is another advantage of increasing your muscle mass (Beaumont, n.d.). Introducing cardio to your workout will actually amplify the rate at which you're burning fat.

Here is some useful advice for remaining steadfast in your weight loss routine (Beaumont, n.d.):

- **Remember that exercise is a lot of work.** Nothing that's worthwhile is easy to achieve, and because of your brain's natural tendency to protect you from things or situations that cause you discomfort, you're likely to hear your inner voice making excuses for why you shouldn't or can't do it. This can be countered by selecting exercises you find enjoyable, so instead of being miserable when the clock strikes and it's time to get to it, you know you'll still be having fun, which can act as motivation to see it through.
- **Don't neglect your strength training.** Yes, building muscle mass is crucial, which means weight training is recommended. However, strength training is what

speeds up your metabolic rate, and this is precisely what you want when trying to lose weight. Strength training is also crucial when you're trying to improve your mobility and range of motion as a senior.

- **Start small if you have health problems.** If your priority is to burn as many calories as possible, but you have health problems or are just starting out, the key is to start small. This means you should walk as frequently as you can and increase your speed and distance as your stamina increases. Individuals that are not at risk may prefer cycling or jogging. It's great for you to have big goals, but you need to prioritize your health, so you don't end up hurting yourself in the long run.
- **Increase weights when building muscles.** If your priority is to build muscle mass quicker, you should reduce your number of reps and increase the load of your weights. For example, instead of using light weights and doing more reps, you'd do fewer reps but with heavier weights. This is a better option because doing more reps with weights that don't challenge your body as much may act as cardio as opposed to mass building.

After learning all the benefits strength training has to offer, you may be eager to jump right in, but you have to keep in mind that you still need the go-ahead from your healthcare provider before getting started. This is simply for your own safety, particularly if it's been a while since you were last physically active.

Once that's out of the way, don't let anything stop you from achieving your health goals, and remember that there is no restriction on who can participate. This workout is for anyone and everyone, and you have the freedom to do as little as 15–30 minutes per session, about twice or thrice a week—whichever works for you! We can often let our age be an excuse as to why we can't exercise fully, but don't let this stop you from challenging yourself.

Who wouldn't want improved joint flexibility, more muscle mass, and stronger bones? (Especially if you're hitting an age where the biology of the human body is clearly telling you it won't be able to keep up with your physical needs if you don't do something about it.) Additionally, you'll get the added benefits of managing your weight more effectively and improving your balance.

HEALTHY AGING

There's no way for us to stop our biological clock, and why would we want to? Growing older comes with many positives, such as experience and wisdom. While our features and physical capabilities change as we age, there's no reason why these changes have to be all negative. The human body is amazing and beautiful in every way and at every milestone of our lives, so rather than fear or reject it, we should welcome and embrace it.

The only way that we can ensure healthy and graceful aging is through good nutrition and regular exercise. While people of all ages are encouraged to exercise, it's especially important as you approach your senior years. I know many may be thinking it's too strenuous for the elderly; however, you couldn't be more wrong. Of course, you're not going to be doing the same kind of exercise you'd do if you were 30 years younger, but regularly engaging in physical activity is essential to your well-being. A senior's regimen may consist only of flexibility and balance training, aerobic exercises, and strength training. Not only that, but it would be a lot milder than a workout done by a 25-year-old (for example).

Don't get me wrong, I'm not promising that doing this somehow stops the natural processes that have to occur as a result of getting older. What I am saying is that the detrimental effects of not taking care of your health in your younger years can be improved. You'll look and feel healthier, as well as be able to do more than your fellow seniors who are not engaging in physical fitness.

Research suggests that physical exercise in seniors reduces your chances of high blood pressure, diabetes, coronary heart disease, and colon cancer (HUR USA, 2019). Individuals with low stamina and chronic conditions will also benefit greatly from this. Nearly all of the most common conditions ailing the elderly can be substantially improved with the addition of a simple workout routine, a few times a week.

CONSIDER YOUR CORE VALUES

When you start pursuing strength training, it's valuable for you to consider your core values. Starting your fitness journey won't be easy because you will come across obstacles. This is why it's important for you to keep your core values at the root of your journey. You will use these values to motivate you and listen to your body when you feel as though you're exceeding your limits.

What comes to your mind when you think of values? You may think of your morals in life that help you to make the right healthy decisions. However, our values are more than just morals we consider when we need to make good choices. Your values play a role in the small everyday decisions you make, whether you realize it or not. Many of us don't realize how influential our core values are each day, which is why it's valuable for us to take time to consider it.

Your core values make up the foundation of your beliefs and opinions. You need to be able to respect your values in order to love and respect yourself holistically. We can often go through life forgetting about our values and the role they have in our lives. This is why it's crucial for you to take the time to identify your values so that you can apply them when making everyday decisions.

Choose and Identify Core Values

Let's start off by identifying the values that mean the most to you and then you can continue to choose the values that would help you the most along your fitness journey. Follow these steps to determine what your core values are:

1. **Create a list.** You can start by creating a list of different values that are important to most people, including yourself. Think about all the general values possible and write them down. You can even look up some general values that people may have, or you can ask someone you're close to. Ensure that this list has many options and don't forget to add all the values that apply to your life.

2. **Pick out the priorities.** Although all the values that you have written down may be valuable, you do have some core values that you value more, whether you're aware of it or not. You need to consider which values are reflected in the decisions and aspects of life that mean the most to you. For example, you may prioritize considering people around you, and this core value is used with every decision you make in your life.

3. **Consider past experiences.** A great way for you to determine what your core values are is by taking a look at your past experiences. Sometimes we are unaware of our thought processes and values when we're in the moment. You could be using your core values every day without you even realizing it! So consider these experiences and how your values aligned with the decisions and behavior you participated in.

We each have our own values in life, so it's important to find out what aligns with your mindset. When you identify and choose what matters to you the most, you'll be able to make better decisions in your life that aligns with your core personality and morals. This will make you a happier and more fulfilled individual.

Create Your Goals

Once you identify what your core values are, you should work toward setting and creating goals that reflect these values. You want to ensure that your objectives throughout this fitness journey align with the values that make you who you are. What do you hope to achieve from this experience and change in lifestyle? You may just answer that question by saying "I just want to get fitter," but you should dig a little deeper than that.

Listen to Your Values

During this fitness journey, you need to listen to your core values. When you listen to your values and stick to them, you will be more successful with your progress and results. Often, when we get so focused on the end goal, we forget to put ourselves first, which can ultimately cause us to limit ourselves. Here are some ways you should ensure that you're listening to your values:

- **Respecting your limitations.** Knowing how to identify and respect your limitations is a good value that every person should have. It's important to challenge and push ourselves, but there comes a time where you need to put your own wellbeing and health first. When you are too hard on yourself, it can result in you overworking yourself, which can increase your risk of hurting yourself.

- **Putting yourself first.** Although it's important to put your health first in any situation, sometimes prioritizing health and fitness can be detrimental. Your morals and values will always allow you to consider your health, safety, and happiness as a priority. You need to get used to putting yourself first on this journey, as it will help you to stay consistent while still giving yourself the rest you deserve.

- **Not giving up.** There will come a time within this journey where you are fed up and tired of exercising. If all you want to do is rest, it makes you feel as though you should just give up. Although it may seem easier to give up, you should take a look at your core values before making an impulsive decision. One of your values may be that you want to remain perseverant, even through the difficult parts. Yes, you must listen to your body and give it the rest it needs, but once you're recovered, it's time for you to get back out there!

Being true to yourself will help you to be successful throughout this journey. As you stick to your values, you're able to be consistent and effective with your workouts. You'll find that you have a happy and realistic fitness journey that gets you the results you desire. Remember to always look after yourself, and you'll get to where you need to be physically!

2

MYTHS AND FACTS ABOUT GETTING OLDER

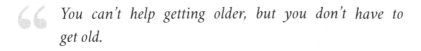 *You can't help getting older, but you don't have to get old.*

— GEORGE BURNS

Getting older has certainly gotten a bad rep as the years have progressed, and some people either fear it or do their utmost to somehow try to delay it. Heck, many people even refuse to accept that they're getting older, so they still behave and dress like they're 20–30 years younger than their actual age.

What would help people accept and welcome getting older is debunking some of the myths responsible for society's misconceptions about the golden years. So let's jump right in!

MYTHS DEBUNKED

When it comes to seniors and exercise, there are a lot of myths that may make you believe that your fitness goals are unrealistic. Seniors are capable of a lot more than people realize. Just because you're older doesn't mean you should lower your standards and fitness expectations. Debunking these harmful myths can help you to live a healthy and fit life that doesn't hold you back. When you believe the myths people tell you about your fitness abilities, you'll never be able to push yourself and discover what you're truly capable of. Every senior is different, so it's wrong to generalize and say what others can or can't do.

"Seniors Can't Drive"

A common misconception about seniors is that they aren't able to drive. Many people generalize and say that older people can't see properly, their reflexes are shot and they're a hazard to anyone on the road. Although there is an exception for this myth, as many seniors aren't able to drive at a certain age, this may not be true for all of them.

As long as you have good eyesight, you wear your glasses, you're alert, you have a fast reaction time, and you can respond to cars around you, there shouldn't be anything stopping you from driving. Many seniors still want that freedom to move around wherever and whenever they want, and you deserve to have it!

"You're Too Old to Quit Bad Habits"

A saying that you've probably heard in your life is "you can't teach an old dog new tricks". Many people assume that once you become a senior your time for doing new things, growing as an individual, and making better choices is over. When you're older, you're still able to grow, develop and make better habits for yourself. This means that you are never too old to quit habits that are hurting you or holding you back! Some of the negative habits that you can leave behind as a senior include the following:

- **Smoking cigarettes.** Have you been smoking cigarettes most of your life, so you see no point in quitting now. Your habit of smoking may have resulted in you having breathing and lung issues, which can provide an obstacle for you along your fitness journey.
- **Overindulging in the wrong foods.** For many of us, food can be our greatest weakness. Sometimes we crave the wrong foods, and it's good to spoil yourself every now and then. But if you don't also fuel your body with the right foods, you can experience various health issues, and this can make your fitness journey even more challenging.

You may think because you're old, you should just give up on trying to be better. You've had your whole life to quit these bad habits, and it's not going to do you any benefit now anyway. When you think like this, you give in to an untrue myth that will influence you to give up on yourself. Just because you're older doesn't mean you're incapable of change.

If anything, now is the time for you to introduce healthy change into your daily routine so that you can make the most of life. Quit all of those toxic habits that are holding you back, so you can flourish physically and mentally. When you let go of these habits, you'll be able to look after your health and this will only benefit you along your fitness journey.

"Exercise Won't Help You"

When you reach a certain age, you may tell yourself that there's no point in trying to be fitter or more active because it won't do anything for you. You believe that your fitness journey is a lost cause and every time you try to push yourself and fail, you use your age as an excuse to give up. As seniors, you're told so often that you won't be fit anymore, but this is far from true.

Although you may be in bad shape at the moment, this doesn't mean you cannot get stronger and adapt over time. We need to get rid of this myth that undermines the strength and capabilities of elders. Exercising regularly will help you in every aspect of your life, even if it takes you some time to get into the hang of it.

"Your Body Can't Keep Up With Your Mind"

As we've established earlier, you will be able to recover your strength and fitness with enough practice and determination. This myth is completely false, as it makes seniors seem as though all you can do is sit around and think. Physical activity is imperative for your mental fitness. When you're moving your body around frequently, it will actually help you to become sharper mentally, as you regain your memory, cognitive thinking, and other mental strengths.

When you put your mind to accomplishing your goals of getting fitter and happier, your body will be able to fulfill these wishes. At first, you may find it really challenging to get active, especially if you are suffering with aches and pains, as well as mobility issues. The more you practice your exercises consistently, the easier it will start to become for your body. Eventually, your mind and body will be in the best shape they have been in a while.

"All Old People Have Arthritis"

Although arthritis is a common condition for older people, it doesn't mean everyone gets it. People like to generalize when it comes to health conditions seniors have. They think that just because you're older, you're bound to suffer with uncomfortable or even life-threatening conditions.

There are various things you can do to avoid getting arthritis in the future. Simply exercising more and looking after your general health will reduce your risk of getting it. If you already have arthritis and you think it will hinder you from exercising effectively, you should explore some water exercises. Doing water aerobics or other forms of water exercises allows you to get your workout in, without having to put any uncomfortable pressure on your joints.

"You Need Anti-Aging Products"

We've been advertised anti-aging creams and skin-care products almost our whole lives. Even as young adults, we're sold anti-aging products that can prevent you from developing wrinkles in the future. Although some of these products may work, they shouldn't be your priority as a senior.

Do you want to look younger, glow, and feel confident again? You're not going to achieve all of this by merely using an expensive cream every day. The best way for you to look younger and feel better is by doing consistent exercise. You don't only *look* more radiant and youthful, but you will also *feel* so much better. You'll be able to do things you never thought you could do anymore. At the end of the day, it's more important to feel good from within than to prioritize how you look.

"Exercising Will Lead to Injury"

You may be more fragile and delicate than you used to be in the past, but this doesn't mean that doing exercise is going to hurt you. If you think that participating in any form of exercise will injure you, then you'll never feel confident enough to begin your fitness journey.

Obviously, there is a possibility of hurting yourself when you don't do exercises properly, you push yourself too hard, and you don't give your muscles enough time to recover. But, if you do your exercises correctly, while looking after yourself, you are very unlikely to get hurt.

All that is important is that you exercise cautiously so that you don't risk getting hurt. If you have any pre-existing conditions, you should go see a doctor so that they can inform you on what your limitations should be. This will help you to know which type of exercises you can do so that you don't end up hurting yourself.

"You Can't Exercise Because of Your Disability"

If you have a disability because of (or unrelated to) your old age, this doesn't mean you are unable to exercise. There are various types of exercises you can do that will cater to your disability. It's valuable for you to consult your doctor so they can let you know what exercises you should do that will be suitable for your goals. Throughout this book we will also explore some seated exercises that you can do, which can be suitable for you and your disability.

"Obesity Is Inevitable"

When you get older, you may find it more challenging for you to lose weight. Your metabolism isn't as fast as it used to be and any negative eating habits you may have had in the past starts to catch up with you. This may make you think that obesity is inevitable in your later years, and you should just accept the weight gain. Although there is nothing wrong with gaining a bit of weight, you shouldn't just expect yourself to get to a dangerous level of weight.

If you stop caring about your weight, keep your unhealthy eating habits, and avoid any type of exercise, you will find yourself at more risk for health conditions and diseases. When you tell yourself obesity is inevitable, you will overindulge in the wrong foods that harm your physical health. You will also find that neglecting your health ultimately makes it more challenging for you to become fitter.

"You Don't Contribute to Society"

Some people treat seniors unfairly, because they don't think they contribute anything valuable to society. This couldn't be further from the truth! Aside from the fact that you've had decades of contributing to society, there are other ways to be an effective member of society, including the following:

- **Supporting small businesses.** As a senior, you're still contributing to businesses by being a consumer. You support small businesses, especially when they are owned by someone you know or care about. Even if you only buy from bigger companies, you're still contributing to the economy.
- **Sharing your wisdom.** As a senior, you have more general knowledge and wisdom than other people. You have the power to teach younger people around you so you can help them to make better decisions and avoid mistakes you may have made in the past. Imparting this wisdom to other people can benefit many younger people, as life can be challenging.

- **Volunteering and assisting with tasks.** Seniors are some of the most helpful and friendly individuals, as they are always caring about others and trying to find a space to help. Whether it be volunteering at your local library to helping and lending a tool to a neighbor, seniors often jump in and help where needed.

Seniors provide so much value to the area that they live without many even realizing it. You have a purpose even in your later years, and you'll be able to accomplish even more when you exercise and boost your overall health.

"You Can't Do Anything You Could in the Past"

A common myth many people believe is that once you reach a certain age, you won't be able to do the things you could do in the past. You may mourn for the activities you used to do, because you think that you are no longer in the position to do them. Just because you're older doesn't mean you can't participate in the same activities you did before.

No one should use their age as an excuse to get out of exercising, because anyone is still capable of fulfilling any exercise they desire. You're able to accomplish anything you want with the right mindset. For example, if you want to get back to playing pickleball or golf consistently because this is what you used to do in the past, you should train yourself and work toward accomplishing this goal.

"Your Heart Can't Handle the Exercise"

When you get older, you may get the impression that your heart isn't as strong as it needs to be. Although your cardiovascular health may not be where you need it to be, exercising will help you to reduce your risk of heart disease, as well as improve the overall health of your heart. This means that you will be more than capable of handling various forms of exercise.

If you're trying to improve the health of your heart, you should practice more cardio such as walking, running, and cardio workout programs. This cardio will gradually improve the overall health of your heart.

"Seniors Don't Need as Much Sleep as Younger People"

We always talk about how important it is for younger people to sleep because they are still growing and developing. You want them to get enough hours of sleep each day because of this. But we don't talk about how important it is for older people to get sufficient sleep as well. In general, every individual should get enough sleep that they can function efficiently.

As a senior you should get more sleep so that you can be at your optimal strength and ability, especially when you're exploring your fitness journey. Sleeping more will help you recover from all of the physical activity you're doing. This will reduce your risk of an injury.

"Alzheimer's Is Inevitable"

Alzheimer's disease is a condition that causes memory loss and disorientation. Although this condition is common in the elderly, it doesn't mean that it's inevitable for every senior. You can reduce your risk of experiencing Alzheimer's by ensuring you look after both your mind and body. Being physically active and healthy can actually boost your memory and overall mental fitness. By constantly challenging yourself and pushing yourself as much as you can through physical exercise and good eating.

"I Can't Exercise Because There's No One to Join Me"

Local community centers have a variety of programs available to all. You can find an exercise buddy there, or have a look at what kind of physical programs they have available. There may be a gardening club or walking group you could join without having to find company yourself. It's possible that there are in-house exercise programs for you to join, too; it only costs that you go check it out. This could be your opportunity to mingle, make new friends—and, who knows, obtain an exercise buddy (Tweed, 2022)!

"The Elderly Are Doomed to Suffer From Loneliness and Depression"

While many people do indeed feel lonely as they age, it's not necessarily a natural part of growing older. Sadness, anxiety and depression only manifest when these feelings of loneliness are prolonged and allowed to worsen. They can severely affect the mental and emotional stability of an individual (National Institute on Aging, n.d.).

"Science Has Provided All It Could Regarding Aging"

Scientists are always making new discoveries, even on matters that were believed to have been properly addressed. This is what gives hope to many older people: the improvement of technology means that, as people live longer, we're able to determine how they can live better. This also means that questions we never dreamed about will start popping up, prompting new tests to be conducted, resulting in new answers.

Be patient with the information that is available to us at this point in time, and trust that as time passes, new information will be gathered that will certainly help treat some of the conditions ailing the elderly. No question is unanswerable.

3

BEFORE YOU START STRENGTH TRAINING

Everything that we do today determines how we're going to live life tomorrow.

— MARTIN DASKO

E veryone has their own physical limitations, which means that you should never hold yourself to someone else's standards. Respecting your body's needs and limits is the only way you'll be able to get the most out of your abilities. Particularly when you get older, you may think that pushing yourself to do more than what you can will build the level of resilience you desire; however, the truth is that you can only do so much. This is precisely why you should listen to what your body is telling you, and focus on consistency as opposed to the amount of strain you're putting your body under.

Now, even with all this extra care you're advised to take when exercising as you age, many of the common conditions ailing the elderly don't prevent them from getting a healthy dose of physical activity. Needless to say, you should always keep your conditions in mind, and follow plans that don't aggravate any of your symptoms. So, the basic gist of this is to not push harder when it hurts.

How much you're able to do will depend on a range of factors. Primarily your bone density, which is why consulting your healthcare provider prior to embarking on your strength training journey is highly recommended. Even if you don't have any direct concerns regarding your health and feel fully capable of doing light exercises, it's in your best interest to obtain a professional medical opinion, just to be safe.

When trying to develop new habits, the key is consistency. This is especially the case with exercise, as it will help with the prevention of muscle tightness. Tight muscles come from inconsistent exercise training, which also increases the likelihood of extreme fatigue and injury.

Intermittent exercise is a driving factor in elevated tenderness and pain. It's commonly known that your muscles are bound to be a little sore when first starting to be physically active. Even though this isn't necessarily the reason why you become more susceptible to injury, it definitely plays a major role in it. Aching muscles may put you off exercising, which is what leads to intermittent exercise, but remember that you're more likely to get injured with stiff aching muscles than you are with muscles that you keep warm and active.

You may even find yourself falling into the category of over or undertraining. Overtraining is possible with inconsistent exercise because, on the days that you finally do decide to exercise, you think you can make up for the time lost, which then causes you to overdo it. Undertraining is exactly what it sounds like— doing too little at a time to make a significant change in your physical abilities, which causes everything to feel strenuous. Both of these can lead to burnout and boost the chance of injury, which is completely counterproductive to your cause.

Inconsistency leads to poor adjustment to movements and a lack of flexibility, which in turn causes strains which could become serious injuries. Your body produces the best results when you slowly but consistently increase the amount of physical activity you expose it to. This will also help reduce risk of fatigue and injury.

Sticking to a consistent exercise regimen elevates your mood, reduces risk of health problems, increases immune system functions, and reduces chronic pains (*The #1 Reason You Need Consistent Exercise*, 2018). The meaning of consistency often gets confused with simply doing something over and over and at the same time; however, in terms of exercise, it refers to increasing the intensity of your training at the pace best suited for your fitness level.

The reason why this is an important factor is because our bodies are designed to adjust to the strain of exercise, so at some point the workouts you're doing will become comfortable, even second nature, and will no longer be beneficial.

Once again, good health and graceful aging cannot be accomplished by doing one thing alone. There are various factors that assist in this endeavor that should be coupled with strength training. These include making significant lifestyle changes.

HEALTHY NUTRITION

A healthy, balanced diet is always the best place to start. Nurture your health starting from the inside. That said, making healthy food choices often becomes increasingly difficult with age. You might feel too incapacitated to cook healthy meals for yourself; your sense of taste and smell may be altered by age, medication, or underlying health conditions; you may find it difficult to swallow or chew certain foods; even your financial situation could interfere with your healthy meal planning (MedlinePlus, 2019).

These aren't the only things that may affect your ability to make healthy food choices, but they're some of the more common ones among older adults. If you are struggling with any of these, reach out to loved ones or healthcare professionals near you for assistance.

Some ideas to help with the issues that might prevent you from eating healthy (MedlinePlus, 2019):

- Consult a dentist for problems with chewing.
- Seek advice from a medical professional if you have a chronic condition or disability that is interfering with your ability to cook or eat.

- Drink sufficient liquids with your meals for problems with swallowing. If it makes no difference, consult a medical professional.
- Incorporate more healthy snacks into your diet during daytime to ensure you're always getting the nutrients you need, especially if you feel you have not been eating enough.
- Exercise in order to stimulate or regain your sense of appetite.
- Organize group meals or cooking sessions if you don't like eating alone. This can be done by checking with your community or senior centers.
- Add texture and color to your meals if you are having problems smelling and tasting your food.

For those who are not burdened with any of the above, start making the necessary dietary changes immediately. The reason why good nutrition is so important for the elderly is the same reason why it's important for all human beings regardless of age: to feed your body the nutrients it needs to function at its optimal level, reduce the risk of certain diseases, maintain a healthy weight, and provide you with all the energy you require (MedlinePlus, 2019).

Regardless of what your diet choices (or restrictions) are— vegetarian, pescatarian, vegan, you name it—As long as you're getting a healthy intake of vitamins, minerals, carbs, proteins, healthy fats, and water, you're giving your body everything it needs to perform at its best.

While elderly folks do require a balanced diet of these nutrients, some individuals may find that they need a higher intake of specific nutrients, for example protein or fiber. This is another aspect of your life where you'll need advice from your medical practitioner, as they are well aware of your nutritional deficiencies (if you have any). Nevertheless, it's a good rule of thumb to steer clear of saturated and trans fats. Trans fats refers to processed fats, while saturated fats are typically animal fats.

Don't get me wrong: Fats are definitely good for you and form part of a healthy diet. However, where you get your fats from is what makes all the difference. This is because unhealthy fats increase the risk of cholesterol. Healthy fats are found in foods like chia seeds, whole eggs, avocados, fatty fish, nuts, and dark chocolate, to name a few (Coila, 2018).

Another essential part of a healthy diet is drinking loads of liquids. Water is ideal, but infused water, herbal teas, and fresh juices are all good choices. It's not uncommon for the elderly to have a diminished sense of thirst, which is what leads many to suffer from dehydration. Also remember that caffeinated beverages—such as coffees, teas, or sodas—can actually dehydrate you, and always balance your intake of caffeine with water.

Many medicines can also contribute to a lack of thirst; however, it's your responsibility not to wait for the sensation of thirst to be present before drinking anything. We'll get into how much water is recommended later on in the chapter, but the commitment to keeping yourself hydrated is the first step.

This will give you the nutrients you need and prevent you from inadvertent dehydration.

You also want to stay away from discretionary or empty calories. This refers to foods that are rich in calories but have no nutritional value. This type of food provides energy; however, it does not contain any dietary fiber, amino acids, vitamins, minerals, and other nutrients. Discretionary calories include store-bought baked foods, candy, soda, chips, alcohol, etc. (MedlinePlus, 2019).

Recommended Foods

According to MedlinePlus, some foods that'll be beneficial to your overall health and fitness are:

- whole grains (brown rice, whole-wheat bread, oatmeal, etc.)
- eggs
- lean meats and poultry
- seafood
- seeds, beans, and legumes
- nuts
- brightly-colored vegetables and fruit
- low-fat or fat-free dairy products (milk, cheese, yogurt, etc.)
- non-dairy milk with added calcium and vitamin D

Fueling your body with the right foods will not only help you to live a healthy life, but it will also improve your performance as you work out.

NUTRITION FOR BONES, MUSCLE MASS, AND STRENGTH

Building muscle mass and getting stronger is about more than just exercising and working out enough, as you also need to ensure that you're getting enough nutrition in your diet. You need to consume the right foods so that your bones can become stronger, your muscles can grow, and you can increase your overall strength and capabilities.

It can be easy for us to neglect nutrition because we forget the role food has in our health and everyday lives. We eat the same things most days and forget about prioritizing nutrients that keep us strong. Although it's valuable for you to focus on your physical fitness, you should also be mindful of your nutrition. You may be taking various pills and potions every day to ensure that you're healthy and consuming the right vitamins, but sometimes the best way for you to get sufficient nutrients into your body is by eating the right foods and prioritizing your diet.

When we say you must put your nutrition first, this doesn't mean that you must hate your relationship with food, cut out all the stuff you love, and eat bland health foods; it just means you must have everything in moderation. Discover what your body needs and enjoys, and provide it with good food—even if you want to treat yourself every now and then.

Consulting a doctor or dietician may help you to realize what you lack from your diet and how you can improve your overall nutrition. Getting an eating plan from a professional may help you to be consistent with your healthy habits, as well as giving you a clearer direction.

Because the deterioration of muscle and bone mass is inevitable as we get older, it's our responsibility to feed our muscles and bones the nutrients they need from a young age. This is particularly important for women, as they're prone to lose more of their bone mass in comparison to men (Coila, 2018). Ultimately, you want to fuel your body with the right foods that strengthen your bones and muscles. This will improve your performance as you exercise.

HYDRATION

As promised, let's discuss hydration in a bit more detail. Hydration is essential to good health. Poor hydration or dehydration increases your risk of urinary tract infections, kidney problems, blood clot complications, heart problems, and heat stroke (NCOA, 2021). Some of these conditions are not that severe, but this is not a matter to be taken lightly, as there are conditions that are caused by dehydration that are fatal.

You can consume all the nutrients from food you want, but without adequate hydration, you're still falling short in terms of your health. The human bodily functions depend significantly on water to heal from sickness or injury, pump blood to the heart, defend against infection, and lubricate the joints (NCOA, 2021).

While we're advised to drink eight glasses of water daily, everyone's hydration needs differ. To ascertain if you're getting enough water, simply have a look at the color of your urine. Adequately-hydrated individuals will notice nearly transparent urine, whereas poorly hydrated individuals will notice dark urine (NCOA, 2021).

Increased Risk of Dehydration in Seniors

Unfortunately, many seniors pass away from dehydration because their bodies require more water, and many of them don't drink sufficient amounts of water during the day. The changes happening within your body as you're older makes you required to drink more water than you used to when you're younger. Another reason why you may be more dehydrated than the average person is because you're taking more medicines each day. The side effects of this medication can often lead to dehydration.

When you get older, you may also find that your thirst and appetite decrease, or you don't feel like eating and drinking as much as you used to. Although your cravings for food and water may have decreased, this doesn't mean you require less of them. If anything, you need to hydrate yourself with more water at this age.

It's especially critical for you to drink more water if you are exercising regularly as a senior. You need to ensure that you aren't getting too dehydrated as you sweat, so you must replace all of the liquids you lose by drinking more water. Otherwise, you could risk hurting yourself during your exercise.

Signs That You May Be Dehydrated

Your body will give you signs when it's in need of water. At the moment, you may not realize that you're dehydrated, but after you drink water, these unwanted symptoms will disappear. To identify whether you're dehydrated, you should be aware of the following signs in your body (NCOA, 2021):

- chronic headaches
- irritability
- reduced cognitive functions
- weakness, dizziness, or general fatigue
- dry mouth
- less frequent urination
- dark-colored urine
- confusion
- cramps in leg and arm muscles

It's imperative that you understand and recognize the signs of dehydration because, while many of the symptoms are simply uncomfortable, others can significantly weaken you and have severe consequences. To make matters worse, dehydration can also lead to poor coordination and exhaustion, which will only increase your risk of falling (NCOA, 2021).

Ways to Stay Hydrated

Staying hydrated can be tricky, especially when you're not in the habit of drinking water regularly. You're so distracted by your other tasks that you forget to drink sufficient water (or you may just be forgetful altogether). You need to find ways to make consuming enough water a daily routine, especially when you're exercising. Drinking sufficient water is even more crucial when you're working out and sweating. These are some ways that you can stay hydrated:

- **Always have water nearby.** The main reason why you may not be drinking sufficient water is because you don't have any water nearby. You forget about it because it's not within your sight. You might find that you're more forgetful than you used to be, which causes you to neglect hydration. You may also drink less water because you don't have the energy or strength to walk around and get water throughout the day. This is why it's valuable for you to get a big water bottle that you keep with you wherever you go so that you can always stay hydrated.
- **Eat foods that contain water.** If you struggle to always drink water, you may want to find creative ways to introduce more water into your diet. There are various foods that have a high water content, and consuming them will help you to hydrate yourself a bit more. For example, you can eat more watermelon or cucumber. These are foods that'll help you to rehydrate without you even realizing it.
- **Drink water with every meal.** Another way for you to remind yourself that you need to drink more water is by having a large glass of water with each meal—make it a habit, as this will get you into the right mindset. It will result in you automatically drinking a glass of

water whenever you're having your breakfast, lunch, and dinner.

- **Add flavor to your water.** Do you dislike drinking water because it's too bland and unenjoyable? If you avoid drinking water for its lack of taste, you can add healthy and natural flavorings to your water so that it's more exciting for you. There are various ways for you to spice up your water. For example, you can add lemon or orange to your water for a citrus taste. For something fresh you can add mint or cucumber to your water.

- **Find a handy way to remind yourself.** If trying out all of the previous tips doesn't help you, it's valuable for you to consider different tips that can help you to put water first. Maybe you can set an alarm on your phone that reminds you every few hours to drink some water. You can let friends or family members you're always around know that you need to drink more water, so they can take the initiative to remind you more.

It's so important to ensure that you're consuming sufficient water every day so that you don't suffer from dehydration. You may not realize that you're dehydrated in the moment, but it will take a toll on you over time. You may find it challenging to get used to drinking more water at first, but the more you force yourself to consume your required daily intake, the easier it will become for you. Soon, you'll be reaching over for your water bottle without even realizing it.

SUNLIGHT

Sunlight is a wonderful way to increase vitamin D levels naturally as well as support the muscles and bones. Another part of our natural functions that takes a dip as we age, is our ability to produce adequate amounts of vitamin D. This is why many elderly folks are being prescribed vitamin D supplements; however, spending at least 30–40 minutes in the sunlight significantly increases the production of vitamin D and is highly recommended to senior individuals.

This is not to say that you should spend hours sunbathing, especially since your skin may suffer the consequences of this choice, but vitamin D is said to start being produced around 30 minutes after exposure to sunlight—so, as long as you're getting regular sunlight, you're sure to be getting vitamin D. I'm not recommending that you no longer take any supplements prescribed by your doctor; I'm simply suggesting an added natural source for vitamin D. This time in the sunlight will likely boost your mood and leave you feeling revitalized. Just be sure to have your bottle of water with you (Sorenson, 2021).

BONE AND MUSCLE STRENGTH SUPPLEMENTS

Supplements are only to be taken at the recommended dosage and under the advice from your doctor. This is for your safety, as some supplements can interact with your medications and worsen your conditions. Once you've gotten the go-ahead from your doctor, you can now incorporate the following supplements into your diet.

Calcium

This nutrient is essential for the health of strong muscles and bones, and is present in many food products such as almonds, dairy products, leafy green vegetables, juices, and calcium-fortified food products. This compound builds bone tissue, reduces blood clots, regulates heartbeat and muscle contractions, and more. Calcium deficiencies can cause osteoporosis in your old age, and rickets in your youth. This is why adults are advised to consume at least 700 mg of calcium daily (Mike, 2018).

Vitamin D

There are various benefits we receive from consuming vitamin D without us even realizing it. One of the main importance of vitamin D is that it has a mutual relationship with calcium. We need calcium, especially as we get older, to make our bones stronger. To experience the benefits of calcium, you must have sufficient vitamin D in your diet, as it helps your body to absorb the calcium.

This vitamin will also help your muscles to grow, and it can reduce your risk of feeling muscle fatigue or experiencing any damage. Having sufficient vitamin D can reduce your risk of getting osteoporosis, so it's strongly advised for seniors to have at least 10 mg a day of vitamin D. You can take supplements that provide you with this dosage, but you can also receive some much-needed vitamin D from sunlight.

To receive your vitamin D the natural way, you would have to spend a reasonable amount of time in direct sunlight. If the region in which you reside doesn't have much sunlight, you will definitely want to continue taking supplements. However, people who reside in sunny regions can reap the benefits of as little as 15 minutes a day. Vitamin D can also be received through certain foods like oatmeal, salmon, oranges, and fatty fish (Mike, 2018).

Collagen

Collagen makes up a bigger part of us than you may think, as mammals have 25–35% of collagen that is found within our bones, skin, teeth, eyes, tendons, joints, ligaments, and organs. It is naturally produced by our bodies, but after your twenties, it starts to slow down. This is why it's so important for you as a senior to ensure you're increasing the collagen you consume, as it can provide you with various benefits and bodily functions.

If you've noticed that your joints are weaker, your skin has lost its firmness, you have weaker or less defined muscles, and the elasticity of your skin is causing wrinkles, then it's time for you to increase your collagen intake. Old age is not the only thing that reduces your production of collagen, as a lack of sleep, stress, and unhealthy habits can impact this bodily function.

Omega 3 Fatty Acids

Omega 3 fatty acids are highly recommended for seniors (unless advised otherwise by your healthcare provider). This is because they are believed to promote adequate blood circulation, which helps prevent stroke, heart attacks, and clogged arteries. It is also useful for reducing symptoms of rheumatoid arthritis, as well as strengthening joints and bones. Additionally, omega 3 fatty acids improve limb flexibility and agility, which is especially useful for seniors suffering from respiratory issues.

Protein

We all need sufficient protein in our diet to feel strong and healthy. When you're embarking on this fitness journey, you're probably wanting to gain some muscle and increase your overall strength. Protein is the building block of your muscles, so you need to consume a sufficient amount.

Inadequate amounts of protein lead to weak muscles, which in turn not only increases your chances of falling, but also slows down recovery. As with most nutrients, it's recommended to have a high intake of dietary protein in your youth rather than starting later in your life. This is essential for good bone mass, and it assists with the preservation of bone mass as you age. According to the London Osteoporosis Clinic, foods that are rich in dietary protein include lean red meat, fish, grains, poultry, and dairy products.

Whether you're a vegan or vegetarian, you must find alternative ways to add protein to your diet. Many people assume that you can only get protein from meat, but there's protein in various other sources of food: For example, nuts, soy products, legumes, eggs, and some grains.

Magnesium

Magnesium is a mineral that helps with the formation of your bone cells. You need to be consuming sufficient magnesium for you to have strong bones. When you lack this mineral in your diet, you are at a higher risk of having brittle bones, which can lead to greater injuries if you find yourself falling or losing your balance. As you get older, your ability to absorb magnesium decreases, so you need to add more of the right foods into your diet. Foods that you can eat to increase your magnesium intake include legumes, seeds, fish, nuts, green vegetables, and unrefined grains.

Zinc

Zinc is a mineral that also contributes to your bone health, which, as we've established, is something for you to prioritize in your later years. Having a lack of bone density and strength can result in serious injuries, which can make you anxious to embark on your fitness journey. When you increase your zinc intake to a sufficient level, you can feel safe and comfortable knowing that you aren't as fragile as you may have thought.

To ensure that you're consuming enough zinc, you should ensure that you're eating poultry, lean red meat, whole-grain foods, and legumes. If these types of food are in your everyday diet, you are probably getting sufficient zinc.

And there you have it: some of the most important nutrients for healthy bone and muscle health, especially during exercise. You want to do everything you can to ensure your bones and muscles can keep up with the strain you're putting them under. It's essential for you to consult your doctor before starting any exercise regime. Feel free to list any concerns you have and be sure to bring up supplements when speaking to your medical provider or personal trainer. Additionally, make a list of things you want to avoid.

Next, we need to choose the right types of resistance band to suit your needs.

4

KNOW YOUR RESISTANCE BANDS

 May your choices reflect your hopes, not your fears.

— NELSON MANDELA

R esistance bands are great for increasing muscles, significantly more than simply doing bodyweight workouts. For adequate muscle growth you have to place your muscles under reasonable tension, allow yourself proper recovery time, and slowly adjust the load your muscles bear. This will lead you to achieve optimal results that you're satisfied with. These bands produce better strength and neuromuscular (relating to nerves and muscles) performance results. Weight training by itself doesn't offer nearly as substantial improvements to things like back squats and bench presses as power resistance bands do. Athletes often use bands to improve their dexterity and pace.

The versatility of this form of exercise is what makes it so ideal for nearly anyone. From the younger folk trying to build more muscle, to the elderly trying to improve their functions, all the way to individuals being rehabilitated from physical limitations. Resistance bands, when used correctly and suitably for the given task, are a terrific way to improve the functions of joints and muscles, as well as offer protection that may not have been present before to those joints. This can often also accelerate healing.

While free weights may produce desired results, at certain points of the workout, some muscles are not working as they should because of insufficient gravity, like the top section of a curled bicep. Because of resistance bands' variable resistance, the muscles experience continuous resistance throughout the entire range of motion, leading to more effective resistance and improving your muscles' ability to adapt.

Another advantage resistance bands have over weights and machine exercises is that they're so much more cost effective. You can actually afford a number of bands without breaking the bank, and because of their size they take up little to no space. They can easily fit in a drawer or storage box in your wardrobe, which means no matter how many you buy, they can all be reasonably stored. The variety of exercises that can be done using a resistance band is another reason why this little gadget is a must-have.

Depending on the band you're using, you can focus on mobility or simply stretching. Power bands are ideal for working on hip and ankle mobility, whereas flat or tube bands are best suited for pre- or post-workout stretches. The intensity level of these workouts will of course depend on your own fitness level and range of motion, so don't feel bad if at first you need assistance from another person. Your trainer or healthcare provider can advise you accordingly on how much you should start with.

The reason why band strength training has increased in popularity and is believed to offer equivalent, or better, results to weight training is because of its limited strain on the joints. Since so many elderly folks are already ailing with joint pain or injury, this is a definite plus. With resistance bands, you will essentially be getting as much muscle stimulus as possible, without the risk of placing too much pressure on joints or already-fragile bones.

Bands apply persistent tension on your body, which means that, instead of relying on momentum to help you out, you're depending solely on your own core balance to stabilize your position throughout the entire workout. This increased stimulation places your muscles' full range of motion under pressure, which is essentially what you want for the best possible workout.

Resistance bands also allow for a wider range of body positions during workouts as opposed to weights, which generally limit you to vertical positions due to their reliance on gravitational force. With resistance bands, that range of positions now includes horizontal planes, which are great when you want to work on things like chest presses without needing a bench.

TYPES OF RESISTANCE BANDS

The assorted kinds of resistance bands are not only about what shape the rubber is or the length and width of the band; it also matters what that specific band is ideally used for. Let's have a look at some of the bands available and what their focus areas are.

Loop Bands (Also Known as Power Resistance Bands)

The length of power resistance bands is standard, at 41 inches long; however, the thickness is what determines the resistance. These are large rubber bands and can form various loops, which benefit you in a variety of ways—like improving push-ups, mobility, and stretching. They are considered heavy-duty and are used in power lifting and cross-training, as well as full-body workouts, warm-ups, physical therapy, cool-downs, body-weight resistance and assistance, and stretching.

Some people also use loop bands in conjunction with free weights due to the extra resistance this provides. A loop band can also be used in pushing and pulling workouts when anchored to a pole, as well as horizontal and vertical positions.

General benefits (Finlay, 2022):

- muscle strengthening
- muscle endurance
- hypertrophy (rebuilding and growth of muscles)
- stability
- flexibility

- mobility
- rehabilitation
- low joint pressure
- fat loss

Specific benefits:

- unilateral movement (movement that's produced by one limb)
- improved balance
- Improved coordination

Rubber Mini-Band

This is the ideal band if you want to work on the stability and strength of your lower body. It's typically made to be used around the legs, and the length and width will vary according to the level of resistance. Usually, they come in sets branded as light, medium, heavy, and extra heavy, which range between 5 and 50 pounds of resistance.

The upper body can also be worked using this band; however, there are specific exercises involved in that. A mini-band is a lot shorter than a power resistance loop band (a heavy duty resistance band), and significantly wider.

For hip and glute activation, the band should be placed right above the ankles or knees. You can also use it to work on shoulder and elbow stability, activate and stabilize your core, and restore and maintain adequate form. This can be achieved through leg extensions, hips thrusts and squats. Mini-bands are also recommended for those working on calisthenics.

You may notice that some mini-bands have fabric covering the band itself. This is simply for extra comfort, as well as to prevent it from rolling up, which is customary with mini-bands that have particularly light resistance.

General benefits (Finlay, 2022):

- muscle strengthening
- muscle endurance
- enhanced warm-ups
- stability
- rehabilitation

Specific benefits:

- promotion and retention of adequate form
- activation and toning of glutes, hips, and buttocks

Tube Resistance Band

Tube resistance bands don't work all of your muscles; however, they are ideal for pressing and pulling workouts, back rows, curls, and shoulder and chest presses. These tubes come with handles on each end and can be anchored to a pole or door. The amount of resistance you get from tube bands depends on the width of the band, and they usually range between 10 and 50 pounds.

General benefits (Finlay, 2022):

- muscle strengthening
- muscle durability
- hypertrophy (rebuilding and growth of muscles)
- rehabilitation
- low joint pressure

Specific benefits:

- improved range of motion
- fat loss

Light Therapy Band

This band is significantly light, and offers resistance between 3 and 10 pounds, which makes it perfect for stretching and improving mobility. This is the primary choice of senior folks who have significant fitness limitations, as well as individuals recovering from injury. Due to its light resistance, people (especially women) focusing on fat-burning workouts or pilates also opt for this band, as it tones muscles and still has substantial burn. Light therapy bands are relatively long, and can go up to 7 feet. They are light and thin, so they don't loop; however, they can be knotted to make a loop. They can also be used for warm-up or cool-down stretches.

Benefits (Finlay, 2022):

- muscle strengthening
- muscle toning
- flexibility
- rehabilitation
- weight loss

Figure Eight Band

These bands are shaped like the figure eight and its resistance ranges between eight to twenty pounds. It can stretch as far as one needs and have soft handles on both ends which makes them extra comfortable to use. It is used to work both the upper and lower body and simulate gym equipment.

Benefits (Finlay, 2022):

- muscle strengthening
- muscle endurance
- muscle toning
- stability
- rehabilitation
- weight loss

CHOOSING A BAND

The key to choosing an ideal band is to select one that suits your level of strength and fitness. Power resistance bands are a popular choice because of their versatility and durability; however, it does depend on the person using it. Different tension levels are usually color-coded, but remember that each brand may have their own colors for certain resistance levels, so speak to a sales advisor if you're unsure. If you're shopping for your bands online, read the product descriptions closely.

People are advised to have three bands at minimum for their workouts, because each muscle group requires a specific level of tension. This is not a necessity; it's simply a recommendation, and doesn't have to be done right off the bat. You can gradually start incorporating all three bands into your fitness routine.

Also, be mindful of the following (Finlay, 2022):

- **Quality**. Thick bands tend to have more durability and this is definitely something you'd want in your band, because it could be annoying when it becomes sticky, and often dangerous if the band snaps: You could be left with a nasty injury, so be sure to look for thicker bands. Do a thorough inspection of the band as there may be hard to spot damage or tears, which will come back to haunt you. Furthermore, it's best to check your band regularly after purchase for any tears or damage, to avoid hurting yourself.

- **Type of material**. A lot of people opt for fabric as opposed to latex, just because it's much more comfortable to use. The fact that this option is available is great, and you shouldn't feel obligated to buy latex bands just because you see people at the gym using them. Fabric ones are just as effective, and are said to offer easier use and even last longer than latex ones. That said, realistically you'd want to have the option of both, because latex is ideal for upper body workouts due to its stretch, whereas fabric bands are ideal for lower body workouts because they don't slide or roll.

- **Added accessories**. This is another one for when you've had some time to get used to your new regimen and would like to try a few new things with your bands. Some bands have added accessories like ankle cuffs, handles, or door attachments, which is always a nice addition when buying a product. Don't be in a hurry to get those additional, though: First start with your basic training.

- **Variety is the spice of life**. This is true in nearly all aspects of life. As you consistently workout, your muscles will tire of the routine and resistance you're continuously doing, which is why it's great to have a range of resistance levels to choose from as you progress. Needless to say, when starting out, you're going to start with relatively light resistance and gradually increase this as your movement, stability, and strength improve. Buying a range of different resistance levels means you'll conveniently have them ready as you gain strength. It may even act as motivation.

It's valuable to try out various types of resistance bands so that you can try out different exercises with them and determine what works best for you.

HOW TO CHOOSE THE RIGHT RESISTANCE BAND LEVEL

Establishing which level of resistance is ideal for you can often be tricky. You shouldn't choose one based on where you hope to be in terms of fitness one day, you should choose one based on where you are in your fitness journey currently. It's very possible that you may not need very beginner bands; however, it's also very possible that you do. After consulting with your healthcare provider, you'll be better prepared to understand what your current fitness level is, and what you hope to achieve in your fitness aspirations, and which exercises you're planning on doing.

It's always best to start with the lowest level of resistance for exercises focusing on small muscle groups, mobility, stretching, and rehabilitation, before moving on to higher levels of resistance, which will focus on larger muscle groups, chest presses, squats, shoulder presses, bicep curls, thrusters, and more.

Let's discuss what certain levels of resistance are good for to help give you an idea of which category you might fall into.

Level One Beginner or Rehabilitation

This band is going to offer you 3 pounds of resistance and is regarded as ultra-light. Level one beginners are not only beginners; they are also individuals who have limited movement abilities, and people who are new to the fitness scene, in need of physical rehabilitation, or barely active in their day-to-day lives.

These ultra-light resistance bands are great for warming up; improving blood flow and mobility; rehabilitating the legs, arms, and back; as well as increasing muscle strength. Ultra-light resistance bands are not only used for level one beginner workouts. Many still use these bands even after moving on to higher levels of resistance, for warm-ups before starting more intense exercises. This improves flexibility during those work-outs, and reduces the risk of injury or sprains.

Level Two Beginner or Rehabilitation

Offering 7 pounds of resistance, this band is also for those just starting out. People who are relatively active may also find this one to be too light, but again, it's great for individuals who haven't been very active in their daily lives and are only beginning to take control of their physical well-being.

Even though you're starting out with these lightweight bands, you can increase intensity as you progress while still making use of the warm-up benefits these bands have to offer. Bear in mind that, regardless of the fact that this band offers only slightly more resistance than level one beginner, if you haven't been moderately active daily, you're advised against starting off with this one. It is only ideal for people who have already made a point to be physically active every day.

Seven-pound resistance bands can be purchased as:

- **X-Over**. Ideal for beginners and intermediates. These bands target smaller muscles in the back and shoulders, as they are designed to cross over. Weights and other bands rarely work these muscles, so X-Over bands are perfect upper-body-focused bands.
- **FitCord original**. Ideal for full-body workouts; commonly used in HIIT (high-intensity interval training) workouts, Pilates, and yoga. Suitable for nearly anyone and everyone.
- **Body sculpting**. These are stackable bands, which many men may actually find necessary to do since the level of resistance is so low. Body sculpting bands are ideal for women (or disabled people of any gender) just getting into resistance training.

Intermediate

Intermediate-level bands offer 12 pounds of resistance, and are regarded as the lightest-weight level in the intermediate resistance category. These bands increase muscle strength and tone, and can help you build muscle if you're lacking.

How would you determine if you fall in the intermediate category? Well, are you active daily? Individuals who fall in this region are those who regularly jog, hike, play any form of sports, or even simply do frequent chores around the house. If this sounds like you, then you may be on the intermediate fitness level, which means 12 pounds of resistance is an ideal number to start with, regardless of your gender.

Intermediate bands can be purchased as:

- **X-Over**. This is a very popular choice due to the smaller muscle groups these bands focus on in comparison to other bands and weights, which reduces the chance of sport injury and pain. Can be used when starting out, and as a warm up once you progress. These X-Over bands are also useful in free weights, crossfit, bodybuilding, and HIIT exercises.
- **FitCord original**. The ideal choice of gyms, fitness classes, and crossfit boxes users. This band is best suited to those already relatively active, and it is compact, which means it can be taken along nearly anywhere you go.
- **Body sculpting**. Another stackable band option and ideal for mid-level resistance.

OTHER IMPORTANT THINGS TO CONSIDER WHEN BUYING YOUR BAND

Just because a band looks good or stretches significantly further than its original length doesn't mean that it will be able to continuously do so without wear and tear. This is why it's important to pay attention to the quality, and even keep an eye out for the manufacturing process. The last thing you want is to use it for a few workouts and then be left with a serious injury caused by a faulty band. If you're opting for latex bands, be sure you check for any signs of damage, and ensure that the latex being used is of high quality.

Resistance bands have various names such as heavy duty bands, 41-inch loop bands, power resistance bands, and pull-up assist bands. They're all the same thing, and their differences lie in their level of resistance. Importantly, heavy duty loop bands all have the same length, which is 41-inches, and the resistance level is then determined by width. These bands are best suited for pull-up assistance, warm ups, stretching, workouts, and mobility, so if your health and fitness allow it, this is one to be added to your collection once you've reached the appropriate fitness level.

Set for Set has a terrific breakdown of what each of their color bands are used for (*What Size Resistance Bands Should I Get?*, 2019). Unfortunately, each manufacturer has their own colors, and the levels of resistance should be confirmed with the relative manufacturer you're buying from, but this is just to give you an idea of how they are distinguished. Also, you can take notice of the dimensions rather than the color, as the focus areas are likely the same given similar dimensions, regardless of brand.

- **Black**. These bands are 0.85 inches wide and focus on small to medium muscle groups for mobility. They provide light pull-up assistance and additional low-to-moderate resistance when using gym equipment. These are ideal for stretching and jumping workouts.
- **Yellow**. These bands are between 1–2 inches wide and focus on small muscle groups for mobility, stretching,

rehabilitation, and preventative rehabilitation. They provide light pull-up assistance and additional low resistance when using gym equipment. They are great for jumping workouts.

- **Blue**. These bands have a width of 1.25 inches and focus on full-body and/or lower body strength and mobility. They provide moderate pull-up resistance, and moderate-to-heavy resistance when using gym equipment. These bands are also great for stretching.
- **Green**. These bands have a width of 1.75 inches and focus on larger muscle groups. They add heavy resistance when using gym equipment, and are ideal for lower body workouts.
- **Gray**. These bands are 2.5 inches wide and add enormous resistance to conventional strength training. Used for strength training of large muscle groups and large combinations of exercises. Best suited for advanced fitness levels, heavy body types, and for those needing significant assistance with muscle building and pull-ups.

How to Adjust Resistance Band Levels

Resistance bands offer suitable levels for everyone. All you have to do is adjust the band to your preference. You can do this by adjusting your hands; however, if you require further adjustment and need the band to be shorter, you can simply tie it at a length that works for you. If you need it to be longer, you can try tying two bands together, but only attempt this if you're absolutely certain it can be done securely; if the bands come untied, they can snap and rebound, and you can get hurt.

But by far the best way to "adjust" the amount of resistance in your band is to control the amount of slack. Pull it tighter for more resistance (or step back further from the anchor point, if you're using one), and allow a tiny amount of slack for less resistance.

By the end of your repetitions, you should feel like you have no more strength to continue. Once you start feeling okay by the end of those repetitions, it's time to increase the level of resistance of your band. If you don't have higher-resistance bands, you can always add to your number of repetitions.

As mentioned in earlier sections of this book, senior folks can benefit enormously from resistance band training, as it helps decrease chances of falls and injury. Even with all the various bands discussed in this chapter, your training and bands will always be adjustable to suit your specific needs and limitations.

Additionally, there's no need for you to use bands alongside other gym equipment (although it is an option). Resistance bands are not only useful for rehabilitating past injuries; they are also perfect for preventing future injuries, because they improve core strength, flexibility, balance, stability, and joint mobility.

Chapter Takeaways

- **Slow and steady wins the race.** There's no rush, and when you rush, you risk the band violently pulling you back. Maintain control over the band as you move back to your starting position to prevent injury and avoid inadequate form. This can be done by working slow and steady.
- **Select suitable levels of resistance.** Never start off with resistance higher than you can manage, no matter what you think you can handle. If you haven't been very active, it is always best to start with the lowest level of resistance and work your way up as you get stronger.
- **Eliminate the slack.** This involves ensuring the band is far enough from you that it is pulled as taut as possible.
- **Make sure your anchor point is secure.** A solid and secure anchor point is essential for your safety. You don't want anything accidentally opening (or, worse, snapping) and hurting you.
- **Add a second band.** This is only when you've reached a point where the band you're using is no longer challenging you.
- **Inspect the band for damage.** Another essential step, as cracks and tears increase risk of bands snapping and causing injury. You'll be putting a lot of tension on these resistance bands, so you want to ensure that they don't end up hurting you. Inspect your bands regularly for cracks or tears.

5

GETTING STARTED

> *One important key to success is self-confidence. An important key to self-confidence is preparation.*
>
> — ARTHUR ASHE

R esistance band strength training isn't just about getting started and pushing yourself as you go along. There are certain elements and key factors that form a successful workout regimen.

As you know, there's not much equipment needed with this form of exercise; however, there are a few additions that can make the world's difference to your workout. Such as:

- **Sneakers**. This is essential if you're going to be working out on a surface where it's possible to slip. Of course, many band workouts can be performed without sneakers—or even without standing, as you'll learn—but you'll certainly want to prioritize your safety and balance, so it's advisable to opt for sneakers.
- **Foam rollers**. These are ideal for loosening up your joints and muscles. This is not a necessity, but many people make use of foam rollers to avoid working out with tight joints and muscles, which is helpful for the reduction of pain.
- **Resistance bands**. The one best suited to your physical abilities and preference is recommended. You can have a few bands with various resistance levels for when you progress and move on to higher levels of resistance.
- **Comfortable clothes**. Your workout clothes play a big role in how you feel as you work out, because heavy clothing often feels like an additional weight as your body begins heating up. Make sure the clothes you've chosen are breathable.

Ideally, when starting your resistance band training, it's best to try and complete at least two 30-minute sessions per week. The sessions shouldn't be consecutive, and can produce more significant results than you think. This is the recommended amount of training sessions for everyone, not only for beginners.

Those who are already at an intermediate fitness level are advised to only increase the level of intensity, rather than the number of workouts too. For individuals incorporating various other forms of workouts, such as cardio, into their regimen, it's best that you schedule your resistance strength training on different days from that workout. Alternating between exercises is going to be the best way to avoid placing too much strain on your muscles.

SEATED AND LYING-DOWN EXERCISES

Individuals with limited movement will be pleased to learn that resistance band strength training doesn't only have to be performed standing up. You can be seated on a chair, or even be lying down, and still benefit from a full-body workout. This is because stretching the band is what works the various muscles, which means you simply have to do a workout that works the most muscles possible. Let's discuss a few of the numerous types of exercises that can be done like this.

Lying down:

Exercise 1. Pecs.

1. To start the workout off we're going to focus on working the pecs.
2. This will be done by wrapping the middle of your band around your upper back as you sit on a yoga or exercise mat.
3. Next, you'll take hold of both ends of the band and lie flat down. Your knees should be kept apart (about the width of your hips), and you can now bend your knees 45 degrees and place your feet flat down on the mat. Your elbows should be pointed out to your sides while kept at a 90-degree angle. Ensure that the band has no slack. You can do this by wrapping the band ends

around your hands until you feel the resistance. This is referred to as the starting position.

4. Now, you're going to slowly move your hands above your shoulders and ensure that they're straight.

5. Hold it there for about 2 seconds before returning to the starting position.

6. Do 8 – 12 repetitions of this exercise. Do 2 - 3 sets.

Exercise 2. Abs, arms, and **back.**

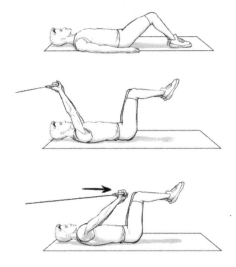

1. For exercises that work your shoulders, abs, arms, and back you can fold your band in half, but be sure there's a decent-sized knot where the band folds.

2. Position the band in a door, closing it at least 2 feet high up from the ground or floor, where the knot will be kept stable.

3. Now sit a few feet away from the door. Ensure your back is facing the door.

4. Next, you should lie back, with your legs bent and feet flat on the ground.

5. Stretch your arms behind you to grab hold of the band ends. You can now wrap the ends of the band around your hands to ensure there's no slack. Your knees and hips should be bent at 90 degrees, and your legs should be lifted to a point where your shins are parallel to the floor.

6. Maintain this position while slowly moving your arms towards your knees and allowing your shoulders to lift from the surface, by a few inches.

7. Return to the starting position.

8. Do 8 – 12 repetitions of this exercise. Do 2 - 3 sets.

Exercise 3. Thighs.

1. This workout is for working your thighs and can be done right after completing your above sets.
2. The band should still be kept in the door; however, each end of the band will now be tied to your ankles. Be sure to face away from the door as you will be lying on your stomach on a yoga or exercise mat, with your legs spread out behind you. Ensure that there is still no slack.
3. Now, with your arms crossed in front of you, rest your head down on them.
4. Slowly bring your heels toward your buttocks while keeping your hips and upper thighs on the mat. Don't stress if you can't reach your buttocks—just bring your

heels as high as you can. Your stomach muscles should be kept tight to reduce risk of arching your back.

5. Bring your feet back to the floor and repeat the movement.
6. Do 10 – 20 repetitions, and 2 - 3 sets.

Seated:

Exercise 4. Hamstrings, glutes, and thighs.

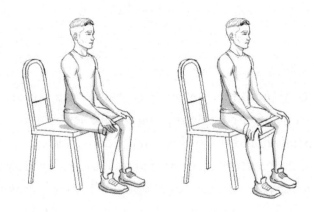

1. For working out your hamstrings, glutes, and thighs, sit down at the edge of a stable chair.
2. Now, place the band just above your knees and separate your legs (part them about the width of your hips).
3. Push outwards and against the resistance of the band repeatedly with your knees.

4. Be sure to keep your ankles stable and bring your knees in line with your ankles.

5. Do 10 – 20 repetitions, and 2 - 3 sets.

GRADUAL PROGRESS IS KEY

It's easy to assume that because it's simply a band, there's very little danger or concern when it comes to overdoing it; however, this is a common misconception. To get the best results, one has to take it nice and slow and increase their intensity, resistance, and number of reps gradually, rather than taking on too much too quickly. Taking on more than you can handle will place you at a higher risk of overuse injuries, like bursitis (an inflammation of bursae, the fluid filled sacs that cushion the joints. This causes pain, swelling and stiffness and the joint) and tendinitis (a condition resulting from inflammation of the tendon, a thick tissue that connects muscles to bones).

So, how will you know if you're overdoing it from the start? Well, a good rule of thumb is to be mindful of whether the movement you're doing feels excessive from the very beginning; if it does, you're not ready for it. The movements you want to give preference to are those that feel fairly easy from the start, and then you can slowly work toward slightly more strenuous movements.

PLAN WORKOUTS ACCORDINGLY

Planning your workouts ahead of time is another important step so that you know which movements you'll be doing next. This allows you to be more prepared, which can help you to have a smooth and speedy exercise, which can be especially beneficial if you are restricted with time. The reason why this is important is to prevent an extensive rest period, which can be detrimental to your health and productivity.

Of course, everyone has their own allocated rest time depending on what their goals are; however, to produce the best results in terms of power and strength, a rest time of 2–5 minutes between reps or exercises is highly recommended. If your goal is improved endurance, then you'd want to opt for a rest period of 30 seconds maximum between reps, and for optimal muscle growth the ideal rest period is usually 30–90 seconds between reps (Barrosos, 2020). Still, you're advised to consult your healthcare provider and personal trainer for advice on this if you're unsure.

Rest periods are determined by the way your body produces energy in order to operate effectively throughout your workout. Though the human body makes use of three energy systems when exercising, how much each system contributes will vary during different phases of the workout, as it depends on the length and intensity of each movement.

EXERCISE SPEED AND TEMPO

You can determine an exercise's intensity by considering its speed or tempo. The speed and tempo of an exercise determine how quickly and intensely you're exercising. When you're considering the speed of your exercise, you are thinking about how fast you're physically doing the motion of your exercise. However, when you're considering the tempo of your exercise, you're taking note of the amount of control or force you're using in each exercise, and how long you place this pressure on your different muscles.

When you're starting off with your exercise journey, you should focus on doing exercises of a slower speed and tempo so that you don't overexert yourself. Once you're fitter, you can increase your speed and tempo so that exercises are more intense and challenge you further.

Concentric, Isometric, and Eccentric Phases

Before we get into the ideal speed or tempo for your workout movement, let's discuss the concentric, isometric, and eccentric phases, as this will help give you an idea of why the suggested methods are best suited.

Concentric Phase

This phase or occurrence is when a muscle is contracted, which shortens the muscle. For example, if you use your arms to curl a weight at a regular quick pace, you're performing the concentric phase.

Isometric Phase

This occurrence only takes place when a muscle is held in a state of contraction for an extended period. If you're curling a weight with your arm, you pause halfway through while holding the weight. This is the isometric phase.

Eccentric Phase

This phase is when the muscle returns to its relaxed or lengthened state, meaning it is not experiencing any form of contraction. You return your arm back to the starting position and you are no longer lifting the weight; your muscles are relaxed.

The key with this section is to understand the importance of starting with easy movements and slowly ramping up. Slow movements are known for building much better strength in contrast to faster movements.

Intense Concentric and Restrained Eccentric Is Best

Building speed and strength using resistance bands is best done using this method. Your concentric movements can be explosive; however, it's imperative that you restrain your movements during the eccentric phase. Resistance bands help make this easier since you have to be mindful of maintaining your form, and rapid releases almost always negatively impact your form.

You may even notice how easy it is to have an explosive concentric phase with bands in comparison to free weights. It doesn't feel as strenuous, yet still produces exceptional results.

The key is to incorporate a decent isometric phase into it (if you can, of course).

For an explosive concentric, squeeze the muscle as you reach the peak, hold, and release slowly during the eccentric phase. This is also much safer in terms of preventing snapback from the band. Additional benefits of this method, as mentioned, are improved muscle strength and mass. This doesn't mean that explosiveness is a necessity.

You should do what your fitness level allows you to do. If you can only do slow, controlled concentric and eccentric phases, then that's what you should do. You will still reap the rewards of your efforts. It is, however, advisable to do your best to incorporate an isometric phase into your workout.

PROPER BREATHING

Proper breathing techniques are extremely underrated, and many people underestimate, or don't understand, the role this plays in a successful workout. Breathing correctly is an important part of strength training and can make a significant difference in your performance and endurance. Controlled breathing allows for a calm workout, which in turn increases your level of alertness and function. It also increases the chance of all muscles being worked, rather than only some, and often helps you lift more than you thought you could (Davis, 2018).

Adequate breathing is also helpful in reducing the amount of carbon dioxide your muscles produce, bettering your heart health and blood circulation, getting the most out of your workout, and decreasing the amount of air you need throughout your routine. It's common for people to inadvertently hold their breath during certain movements of their workout. However, you're strongly advised against this, because it poses many health risks like muscle cramps, hernias, nausea, lightheadedness, and sometimes even heart attacks (Davis, 2018).

The reason for this is because holding your breath is basically robbing your body of the oxygen it needs. When you hold your breath, your blood pressure increases. Knowing how and when to breathe during your workouts is imperative, because proper breathing allows for better relaxation and balanced blood pressure. You can practice breathing techniques before starting your workout and then incorporate them into your workout.

The most ideal breathing pattern is to breathe in through the nose during the eccentric phase, and then exhale through the mouth during the concentric phase. For instance, let's say you're doing a pushup; you will breathe in deeply and slowly as your elbows bend, and breathe out as your elbows straighten up again (Davis, 2018).

Advice for Perfecting Your Breathing

Use your cool-down periods to practice how to inhale and exhale evenly and consistently. You can do this by extending your exhales to 5 seconds and inhales to 5 seconds. This slow, deep breathing activates the parasympathetic nervous system, which is responsible for feelings of relaxation and promotes recovery and digestion. You can also practice your breathing when doing your warm-up stretches. This helps you shift between rest and activity with ease (Davis, 2018).

WARMING UP AND COOLING DOWN

Few people know that warm-ups and cool-downs should be a part of your exercise routine each time you work out. This is because these activities, though less intense, help you to approach each exercise with more strength and preparation. Both cool-downs and warm-ups work because you're slowly increasing your heart rate, raising your body temperature, and improving blood flow throughout your entire body, which is exactly what your body needs to get ready for the strain it'll be enduring.

To ensure you have the lowest possible risk of muscle soreness, warming up is highly recommended. These pre-workout movements are not only about maximizing the amount of oxygen your muscles get and optimizing your performance; they also help you mentally prepare for your workout. Stretching improves the communication between muscles and nerves so you will definitely have better flexibility.

Cooling-down exercises work in a different way, as they help your heart rate and other functions return to a normal pace after being accelerated during your workout.

Let's have a closer look at warming up and cooling down to ensure we understand what each does to the body, and what type of movements can be regarded as warm-ups and cool-downs.

Warming Up

We already know that warm-ups are good for reducing the risk of sore, aching muscles, as well as injuries. When muscles are stiff you have a higher chance of falling or hurting yourself, thus putting you out of action for a number of days, and that is something you definitely don't want. Any prolonged time off working out is detrimental to your fitness goals.

You don't have to take a significantly long time to warm-up, as long as you're dedicating a few minutes toward getting your blood flowing. If you're going to be doing a longer and more intensive exercise, you can make more time for warm ups.

According to the NHS (National Health Service), some effective warm-up exercises for you to try out include the following:

- lunges
- jogging on the spot
- squats
- arm swings
- walking up and down a staircase
- rapid side-steps
- speedy walking
- cycling
- dynamic stretches

And, according to the Tri-City Medical Center, benefits of warm-ups include:

- **Reduced risk of injury**. You may be wondering how warm-ups have the ability to prevent injury, and the answer is quite simple: Because warm-ups loosen your joints and muscles, they not only prepare you for the exercise, but also decrease the likelihood of twisting, tearing, and ripping your muscles.
- **Enhanced muscle response**. This means your muscles will relax and contract much faster than if you don't warm up. Ultimately, it will allow your muscles to perform more efficiently during your workout.
- **Better blood circulation**. Warm-ups are perfect for improving blood circulation because better blood flow means your skeletal muscles receive more oxygen. Increased oxygen leads to better muscular performance.
- **Psychological preparation**. When you're getting started with an exercise, you may find that you're not actually mentally prepared for it. Warming up can introduce yourself to exercise gradually and safely.

Cooling Down

Cooling down can take anywhere from 5–10 minutes, depending on how you feel (NHS, 2020). Cool-downs are advisable to do in a gradual fashion as opposed to an abrupt one.

These can include going from:

- running to jogging
- fast-paced swimming to slow-paced swimming
- jogging to brisk walking (NHS, 2020)

When you exercise, you will find that your heart rate and blood pressure increase significantly. Practicing some cooldowns can help bring your heart rate and blood pressure down, as well as it can return your muscles back to a more relaxed state. You are reducing the intensity of your movements to cool down your body.

Regularly practicing your cooldown exercises will help your body to recover from exercise, especially when you're doing a more intense form of activity. Cool-downs can only be beneficial for your body, and you'll experience these positives in the following ways.

Cool-downs decrease your risk of Delayed Onset Muscle Soreness (DOMS). This is not to say that your muscles won't be sore after a workout, since that is completely normal. However, DOMS is important when you experience substantial amounts of muscle pain which can be so severe that it interferes with any future exercises. In order to ensure your muscles aren't too painful and recover quick enough for your next workout, cooling down is a pivotal part of the process.

You will only be able to achieve better recovery when you are doing your cool-downs after each workout. It's common for lactic acid to accumulate in the body when doing intense workouts and it can take a while for our bodies to work it out. This is why cool-down movements are useful, as they promote the removal of lactic acid, which in turn accelerates the recovery process. Being able to recover quicker allows you to be more consistent with your exercises, which ultimately allows you to see more results.

Practicing cool-downs regularly will only improve your recovery time, which allows you to do more exercises without straining your body. You will have more productive workouts because your muscles are strong and healthy.

Dangers of Inadequate Warming Up and Cooling Down

Failing to properly warm up or cool down can have negative effects on your body and may even create new health risks. Below are some of the most common consequences of inadequate cool-downs and warm-ups.

Overworked Cardiovascular System

You may be concerned about working out because you worry about your blood pressure and heart rate being too high. Doing sufficient warm-ups and cooldowns ensures that you're looking after your cardiovascular health. If you jump right into an exercise without warming up, your blood may not have enough oxygen, which can put your lungs and heart under a lot of stress.

Without having proper blood flow before an exercise, you can even risk damaging your muscles, which can set you back on your journey toward fitness. You need to use warm-ups to get your body prepared for the intense workout you're going to perform (Tri-City Medical Center, n.d.).

Heightened Risk of Injury

The Tri-City Medical Center informs us that more than 30% of injuries presented to sports medicine clinics are related to damage to skeletal muscles (Tri-City Medical Center, n.d.). Such injuries can be prevented if you perform proper warm-up and cool-down exercises.

Blood Pooling

As we established in the previous danger of neglecting warm-ups and cool-downs, you may experience heart health issues such as blood pooling. If you abruptly end your workout on an intense exercise without practicing some cool-downs, your blood pressure may be too low, restricting its travel to your heart and brain. Ultimately, this can leave you feeling very dizzy and light-headed, and in worst case-scenarios, you could end up falling and hurting yourself (Tri-City Medical Center, n.d.).

6

RESISTANCE BAND EXERCISES

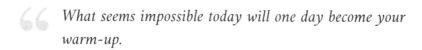

What seems impossible today will one day become your warm-up.

— UNKNOWN

Although we've briefly discussed some of the different kinds of exercises to try using resistance bands, we will now zero in on different muscle groups, specific exercises for those groups, and the exact ways to perform them. This is simply to help you get started without having to do additional research.

NECK AND SHOULDERS

Due to the way we sit and move around in our everyday lives, we may experience more neck pain. If you are at a desktop frequently or you were during your working days, you may be guilty of bad posture. Spending hours on your cell phone can also cause neck and shoulder pain from leaning over too much. This is why it's so important for us to prioritize neck exercises. When you do these neck and shoulder exercises you will find that the pain decreases significantly.

Neck pain may not seem like such a severe problem; however, it can significantly affect your productivity when performing simple daily tasks. These are some exercises for your neck and shoulders (Fit, 2021):

Exercise 5. Shoulder press.

1. This exercise begins with standing upright on the resistance band and holding each end of the band in both hands.
2. Pull the band up to your shoulders, ensuring your elbows are kept out to your sides.
3. Straighten both your hands above your shoulders. However, if this feels too strenuous, you can alternate between hands rather than doing them simultaneously.
4. Start off by doing 7 – 15 reps. Do 2 – 3 sets of this exercise.

Exercise 6. Scapular retractions.

1. Poor posture is a result of weakened tissues in the tendons, ligaments, and muscles connecting the arms to the scapulae. This debilitation causes pain in the shoulders, upper back, and neck. This exercise involves looping the band around your wrists and keeping your arms at 90 degrees.
2. Have your palms faced toward each other and point your fingers up.
3. Next, you will contract your core muscles and gradually turn your elbows to the outside and push your shoulder blades toward each other and hold for at least 2 seconds.
4. Release and bring your arms back to their original position. Your stomach should be tucked throughout,

and your back straightened. Take care to not allow your back to arch.

5. This movement can be done twice or thrice, with a rest period of 30–60 seconds.

6. Each set should consist of 10 to 15 repetitions. Do 2 – 3 sets.

Exercise 7. Modified chin tucks.

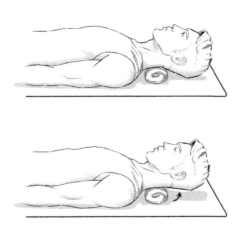

1. This movement begins with laying on your back. You can use a rolled-up towel under your neck at the base of your skull for support.

2. Your starting position will be looking up at the ceiling. From here you will lift the base of your head and bring it down in a fashion that creates a double chin. As if you were trying to look at your feet. Hold this for 5 – 10

seconds. Be sure to keep your shoulders stable. And don't lift your head or neck off the surface you are laying on while doing this exercise.

3. Now, relax your neck and head and bring it back to the starting position where you are looking up at the ceiling.

4. Do this exercise 10 times.

Exercise 8. Tabletop.

1. You're going to drop to your hands and knees as though you're a tabletop.

2. Next, secure the band around the back of your head and hold each of the ends down with your hands on the floor.

3. Lift your head up and push it back; this movement should lengthen the neck. You can now move your shoulders back and when you can't pull it any further, hold that position.
4. Move your head slowly up and down 5 – 10 times.
5. Now, move your head slowly side to side, being careful to not allow your band to slip.

Exercise 9. Lateral flex.

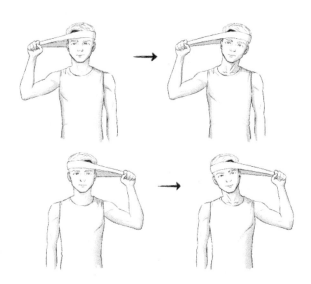

1. Slow, lateral neck movements are a good way to strengthen all the muscles of the neck. The resistance band is added to put slight pressure on the neck to improve the outcome.
2. Put the band over the top of your head as if you are wearing a headband. Insure it is secured and you are

holding the slack of the band with your right hand. There should be some slight tension.

3. Move your head to the left as you hold the slack of the band with your right hand. Hold this position for 10 – 15 seconds and then relax the tension of the band and move your neck back to the starting position. Do 3 sets of this.

4. Now switch it around so you are holding the slack of the band with your left hand.

5. Move your head to the right as you hold the slack of the band with your left hand. Hold this position for 10 – 15 seconds and then relax the tension of the band and move your neck back to the starting position. Do 3 sets of this.

It's important to remember that your neck is sensitive, so you shouldn't push it too far when you're feeling pain. You should also ensure that you're doing your stretches, warm-ups, and cool-downs when it comes to your neck and shoulders. You don't want to strain a muscle or ligament.

SEATED EXERCISES

It goes without saying that some individuals may have a harder time with standing workouts, so this section covers a reasonable amount of exercise you can do whilst seated. These exercises still offer amazing fitness benefits without the strain on the lower body. Here's some you can explore (Mike, 2021):

Exercise 10. Row.

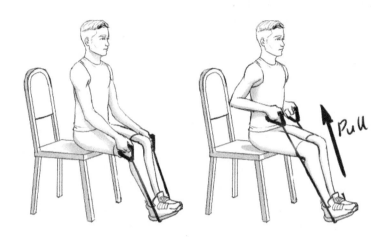

1. The row is for improved posture as it works the muscles of the upper back. You're going to sit on a chair and straighten your legs, but still keep your knees slightly bent.
2. Now wrap your band under each foot and grip each end of the band in both hands. Remove the slack in the band by bending your elbows to 90 degrees. This is your starting position.
3. Move your elbows past your body by slowly pulling your band toward you, and lightly squeeze your shoulder blades inward and downward. Like you are rowing a boat.
4. Bring your arms back to the starting position.

5. This movement should be repeated between 8–15 times in sets of 2 to 3.

Exercise 11. Chest press.

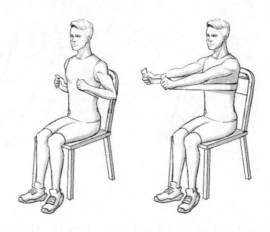

1. This movement is aimed at working the muscles at the front of your body. You can start by sitting in your chair with your back completely straightened and your buttocks all the way to the back.
2. Wrap the band around you from the back, securing it at chest's height.
3. Now, secure each band end in each hand and begin your movement with your elbows bent and your hands as close to your chest as possible. This is your starting position.

4. Next, you're going to gradually straighten your arms out in front of you, while maintaining good posture and form.

5. Bring your arms back to the starting position. This movement should be repeated between 8–15 times in sets of 2 to 3.

Exercise 12. Lateral raise.

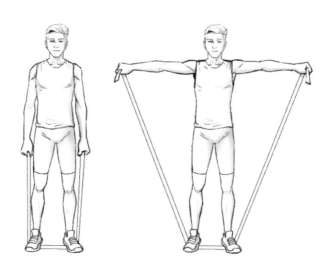

1. This movement focuses on the shoulder muscles and for this one you're going to need a flat resistance band. Secure the band by placing both feet in the middle of the band and hold on to each end with each hand. This is your starting position.

2. Bring your hands up along your sides slightly above your shoulders. If placing both feet on the band creates

too much resistance, you can alter the level of resistance by using only one foot until you're comfortable with the movement, and then moving on to both feet. Your elbows can be slightly bent; however, not too much.

3. Return to the starting position.

4. Do 2 sets of 5 – 10 reps. You can increase the resistance level of the bands as this gets easier.

Exercise 13. Leg press.

1. Leg presses focus on the glutes, hamstrings, and quadriceps. You're going to be lying down for this one, facing up.

2. Now, wrap your band under one foot and start off with your leg in a bent position.

3. Next, you're going to gradually straighten your leg out in front of you and then return to the original position.

4. This movement can consist of 2 - 3 sets for each leg and 8–12 reps should suffice for the beginning stages. Remember that these numbers are simply suggestions to act as a guideline, and you should start with what you know you're capable of comfortably doing.

Exercise 14. Calf press.

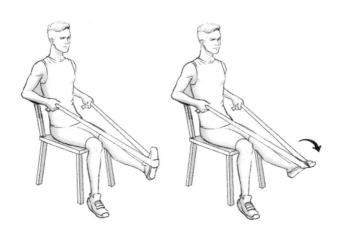

1. On your chair, sit with proper posture and straighten one leg. The band can now be wrapped under your toes, and the ends of the band held in each hand. Be sure that there is no slack to it and hold that position.

2. Lightly push your toes downward and away from your body, creating more resistance in the band. Return to the original position and repeat.

3. Do 2 – 3 sets of 8 – 12 reps.

4. Switch to the other leg and repeat the above steps for that leg.

Exercise 15. Hip thrusters.

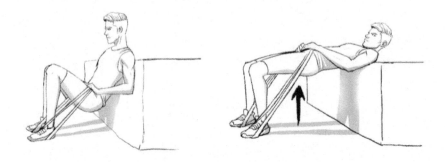

1. You're going to need the looped band for this movement, and rather than sit on a chair, you'll need to move to the couch for added comfort.

2. Double up the resistance band and step with each foot inside the small loops on each side.

3. Place your back on the sitting cushion of the couch. This means your lower back, buttocks, and pelvis are off the couch, whereas your upper back and shoulders are resting on the couch. Pull up the middle of the band to your hips and place it there.

4. Ensure your feet are in line with your knees. Now, push your hips up as high as you can. Don't worry if your knees spread a bit, as this is normal. You're going to

move up and down, and when you reach the highest point, squeeze your butt cheeks and hold for a few seconds.

5. Return slowly down until your butt is just over the floor.

6. Repeat this movement for 5 – 15 reps for starters. Do 2 – 3 sets.

Exercise 16. Knee raises.

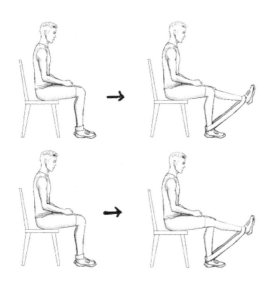

1. This movement should be done using the looped band. It works the quads and hip flexors. Your hip flexors are a group of muscles near the top of your thighs that are key to moving your lower back. They let you walk, kick, bend and swivel your hips.

2. To start, sit on the edge of a chair and wrap your band around your ankles. This movement involves working one leg at a time so hold the leg that is not being worked nice and still.
3. Now, stretch your working leg out in front of you, squeeze as you hold it out for a count of 3 seconds and bring it back down.
4. Repeat this 5 – 15 times.
5. Now switch to the other leg and do the same.
6. Do 2 – 3 sets of this exercise.
7. Feel free to lean a bit back in your chair to make the movement a bit more comfortable to perform.

Exercise 17. Shoulder external rotators.

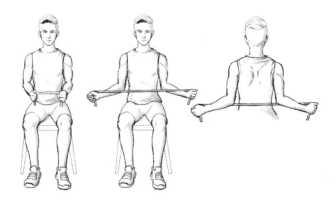

1. This movement works the muscles of the upper back.
2. Sit your chair and hold each end of the band in each hand, removing most of the slack in the band.
3. Start with your elbows bent at your sides at 90 degrees.
4. Now, stretch the band to your sides while keeping your elbows close to your abdomen. As you do this movement, squeeze your shoulder blades inward and downward, hold, and then gradually release and return to the original position.
5. Do 8 – 12 reps and 2 – 3 sets.

Exercise 18. Seated Bicep curls.

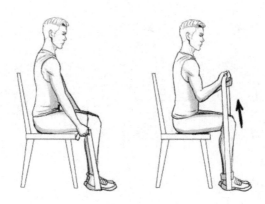

1. Sit upright in a chair and step on the band with one foot. If you're using a loop band you can do it one arm at a time; however, if you're using a flat band, place your feet in the middle of the band and grasp tightly onto the ends. This is your starting position.
2. Bring your hands up to your chest without shifting your elbows away from your body. Ensure that your back is straight, and your shoulders and elbows remain secure.
3. Return to the starting position.
4. Do 5 – 15 reps and 2 – 3 sets.

Exercise 19. Pull-aparts.

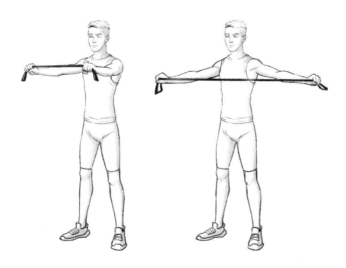

1. This movement works the muscles of your upper back and shoulders.
2. You're going to use the flat band for this and grip the band with your arms out in front of you, either underhand or overhand—whichever is more comfortable. Keep your elbows slightly bent. This is your starting position.
3. Now, stretch your arms out to your sides, allowing the band to touch your chest area, and bring your arms back to the front slowly. Be sure to squeeze your shoulder blades when your arms are fully stretched out, and hold for tension. If the resistance is too much, try gripping closer to the edges of the band for easier movement.

4. Do this for 8 – 12 reps and 2 – 3 sets.

Exercise 20. Shoulder press.

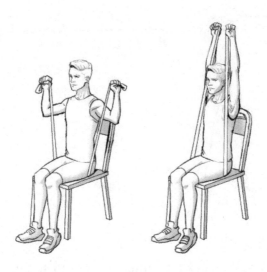

1. The Shoulder press works out the muscles in your shoulders.
2. Hold both sides of the resistance band and sit on the middle section, with both ends still in your hands. Ensure that the band is firmly placed under you, so it doesn't move or slip out when you start this exercise. This is your starting position.
3. Once you're seated upright with the resistance band secure, you can lift your arms with the bands in your hands. Extend your arms straight up over your head.
4. Hold for a second and then return to the starting position. This works out the muscles in your shoulders.

5. Do 8 – 12 reps and 2 – 3 set of this exercise.

These are a combination of simple seated exercises that you can accomplish with your resistance band. You can work out most of the muscles in your body, despite being seated. Choose different seated exercises that engage the various muscles in your body so that you get a full body workout that strengthens all of your muscles.

UPPER BODY EXERCISES

If you want to do exercises to focus on your upper body, these are the resistance band activities that are most suitable. You'll be targeting your arms, shoulders, and torso. Improving your upper body strength can help you to be overall fitter, which helps you to fulfill everyday activities. These are some resistance band exercises you can use for your upper body (Estrada, 2020):

Exercise 21. Triceps press.

1. For this exercise, we will target your triceps.
2. Stand up tall and place the middle of your resistance band underneath your right heel. Hold both ends of the resistance band with your right hand behind your right ear. This is your starting position.
3. Pull your right hand up above your head. Pause for a few seconds and return back to the starting position.
4. Repeat this 8 – 12 times.
5. Now switch to your left side. Place the bands under your left heel. Use your left hand with the bands behind you and next to your left ear.
6. Pull the bands as you raise your hand up above your head. Pause for a few seconds and return back to the starting position.

7. Repeat this 8 – 12 times on the left side.
8. Do 3 sets for each arm.

Exercise 22. Lateral shoulder raise.

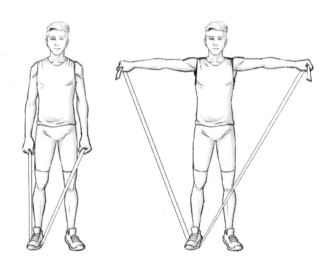

1. This exercise will help you strengthen both your shoulders and your core.
2. Place one foot on the middle of the resistance band. Start this exercise with your hands by your side, holding onto both sides of the resistance band.
3. Start to raise your arms outwards until your hands are at the same level as your shoulder. Your body should be formed in a "T" shape.
4. Return to your starting position by lowering your arms slowly until they are again by your side.
5. Do 8 – 12 reps and a set of 2 – 3.

Exercise 23. Forward raise.

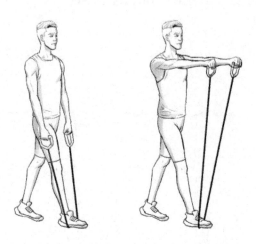

1. This exercise will help you strengthen both your shoulders and your core. You will be doing a different movement then the Lateral shoulder raise. But the starting position is the same.
2. Place one foot on the middle of the resistance band. Start this exercise with your hands by your side, holding onto both sides of the resistance band.
3. Gently lift your arms out in front of you until they are level with your shoulder.
4. Return to your starting position by lowering your arms slowly until they are again by your side.
5. Do 8 – 12 reps and a set of 2 – 3.

Exercise 24. Chest press.

1. This exercise is targeted to your chest. To start, you need to find a solid anchor that can hold the resistance band back for you. Ensure that the band is extremely secure on an anchor like a sturdy pole, because you don't want the band to slip and snap back at you.
2. Once secured, hold each side of the band in either hand with your back to the anchor point. You will be pulling the resistance band away from the anchor point. This is your starting position.
3. With your arms at chest level, start pulling the resistance band until your arms are fully extended. Hold this position for a second or two.
4. Slowly bring your arms back to the starting position.
5. Practice this motion for 10 repetitions and 3 sets.

Exercise 25. Standing Bicep curls.

1. This is a simple resistance band activity that works out your biceps.
2. Start by standing with both feet on the middle of the resistance band, ensuring that it's secure. Hold both sides in your hands and start with your hands at hip level. This is your starting position.
3. Start to lift your arms to your chest in a curling motion, as if you're curling weights. Ensure there is tension in the resistance band, so you work your muscles.
4. Slowly bring your arms back to the starting position.
5. Repeat this motion 10 times for 2 to 3 sets.

You may notice that some of these exercises are similar to the seated resistance bands exercises. Although you can work out your upper body while seated, you should challenge yourself by standing up (if you can). When you practice these resistance band exercises standing up, you'll be able to engage your core and improve your balance.

LOWER BODY

Now let's move onto your lower body. When you tackle your lower body, you have to be standing for these resistance band exercises. You may find them to be more intensive and strenuous on your body, but improving your lower body strength is so important as a senior. Having increased lower body strength will improve your overall mobility and fitness. Here are some resistance band lower body exercises that we will be exploring (Bugden, 2020):

Exercise 26. Squat.

1. Staring off with a very common exercise that we all know about, which you've probably practiced before, we're doing a squat. But this isn't just any ordinary squat, as you're using your resistance band to enhance the workout.
2. Start by standing in the middle of the resistance band with either side of the bands in each hand. You can keep both hands at your side, ensuring there's resistance in the band. If you're trying to push yourself a little more, you can pull your hands up to shoulder level.
3. Slowly squat down with your buttocks pushing back and your knees bent forward.
4. Stand back up to your starting position.
5. Repeat this 10 times for 2 to 3 sets.

Exercise 27. Hip extension.

1. For this exercise, you're focusing on your glutes and hamstrings.
2. Go near a stable heavy object so that you can wrap your resistance band around it. Then wrap the resistance band around your ankle. You want to make sure the band is secure during this exercise so that it doesn't slip off and hurt you as you practice it.
3. Once you're secure, you can start the leg extension by keeping your other leg firm and slowly extend your leg with the resistance band backward. As you extend your leg backward, you must ensure your glutes are engaged and pause.
4. Return back to the starting position.
5. Do this exercise for 10 reps and do 2 to 3 sets.

6. Repeat the same process for your other leg.

Exercise 28. Lunge.

1. You probably know how to do a simple lunge, but the leg exercise we'll be exploring today is the traveling lunge.
2. You start off by standing tall with the middle of the band under one of your feet, while you hold each end of the band in each hand, with your hands at chest level.
3. Take a big step forward with your leg that's holding the band.
4. Then bring your feet together. When you step forward, ensure that you're keeping your knee bent and you're not leaning your body forward.
5. Do 10 lunge traveling steps on each leg for 2 sets.

Exercise 29. Scissor toe tap.

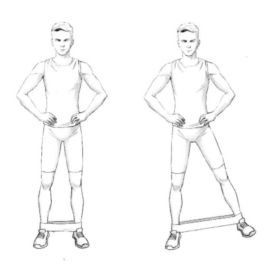

1. In this exercise, we will be targeting your hamstrings and hips.
2. Start by looping your resistance band around your ankles securely, keeping your feet hip-width apart.
3. Step back with your left foot, ensuring that your hips remain facing forward.
4. Hold this position, as you feel the tension in your hamstrings.
5. Bring your foot back to the starting position after a few seconds.
6. For each leg, do 10 reps for 2 to 3 sets.

Exercise 30. Leg press.

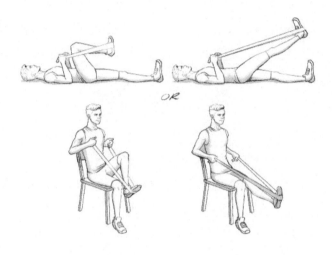

1. You may have heard of or used a leg press machine in the gym. This is a strength training machine that engages your leg muscles, as you push a certain amount of weight. You can perform a similar leg press exercise at home with the use of your resistance band.
2. You can do this exercise seated or lying down. Wrap the resistance band underneath your one foot, while your knee is bent. Hold on to both sides of the band. This is your starting position.
3. Strengthen out your leg with the resistance band and feel the tension in your leg.
4. Return to the starting position.
5. Practice this motion 10 times on each leg for 2 sets.

Exercise 31. Calf push.

1. With leg workouts, we can often forget about our calves. This exercise targets your calves, and it has a similar formation to the previous exercise, the leg press.
2. Start this exercise seated, with your legs extended so they're straight. Wrap the resistance band around the bottom of your feet and hold the ends of the band in each hand. Your heels should be anchored to the ground. This is your starting position.
3. Start to point your feet away from you, ensuring you feel the tension in your calves.
4. Return to the starting position.
5. Repeat this motion 10 times for 2 to 3 sets.

Exercise 32. Glute bridge.

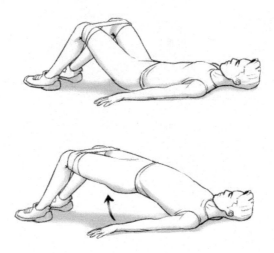

1. As you can most likely gather, we will be targeting your glutes in this exercise.
2. For this exercise, you must start by lying down on your back on a comfortable surface. Your feet should be flat on the ground, with your knees bent. Wrap the resistance band around your thighs, with your feet hip-width apart.
3. Lift your hips and buttocks off the ground slowly. Hold your position for a few seconds. ensure your hips are in line with your thighs. Clench your glutes as you get to the top.
4. Lower your hips back down.
5. Repeat this motion 10 times for 3 sets.

Exercise 33. Lateral band walk.

1. This is an exercise that requires you to stand. Place your feet firmly on the ground, shoulder-width apart. Place the resistance band just above each ankle and wrapped around both legs.
2. Ensure that the band is tight as you stand there. You may have to use a smaller resistance band or tie yours to adjust it.
3. Ensure that your legs are slightly bent, and your leg muscles are engaged. You will be in a half-squat position. This is your starting position.
4. Keep your feet in line with your shoulders and face forward with your body weight evenly distributed over both feet.

5. While maintaining the half-squat position, take a step to the right with your right leg, and then move your left leg to the right as well to form your starting position.
6. Do several side steps, feeling the resistance in your legs as you move.
7. Then perform the same exercise for your other leg by moving to the left.
8. Do 8 – 10 side steps to the right and then 8 – 10 side steps to the left. Do 2 – 3 sets on each leg.

Exercise 34. Back leg raise.

1. Stand up straight with your resistance band around your ankles.
2. Place your hands on your hips or hold onto a chair or sturdy object for balance. This is your starting position.

3. Extend your right leg out behind you while you bend slightly forward. You will feel the resistance of the band.
4. Ensure that you're keeping your hips straight and not twisting them. You should keep your shoulders back and bend your knees slightly.
5. Return to the starting position.
6. Repeat this leg raise 8 - 10 times for each leg. Do 2 – 3 sets.

Because working your lower body can be so intense, we suggest dedicating a day or two of your weekly workout routine to your legs, instead of practicing these leg workouts every active day. Your leg muscles need to rest so that they can recover from this intense resistance band workout.

HANDS AND WRISTS

Doing exercises for your hands, wrists and fingers may seem silly because they're such small muscles in your body, but these are body parts you use on a daily basis for pretty much any task you perform. Unfortunately, when you get older, you may find that your grip, strength, and ability in your hands decreases. This is a common aging obstacle seniors face.

You can eliminate this issue, or prevent it from happening anytime soon, if you practice some simple hand and wrist exercises. They may seem really easy and pointless, but when you practice them regularly, you will find that performing everyday activities becomes a lot easier and more manageable. There are various hand exercises you can do to improve your strength and grip ability, but for these exercises we'll be exploring different activities you can do with a hand resistance band (NHS 24, 2019).

Exercise 35. Hand clench.

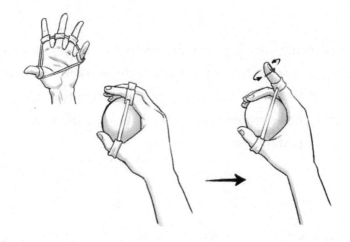

1. Place the hand resistance band on your fingers and hold onto a tennis ball.
2. Start squeezing the ball and ensure that you're gripping with the bottom of your fingers, rather than the tips of them. Maintain the grip of the tennis ball, and slowly lift one finger off the ball until you feel tension on the resistance band.

3. With the finger lifted, start to circle it clockwise, then counter-clockwise. Ensure that you're still gently squeezing the tennis ball as you do it.

4. Once you're done with this finger, you can lower it and move onto the next finger.

5. Practice the same steps on each finger on both your hands.

Exercise 36. Thumb stretch.

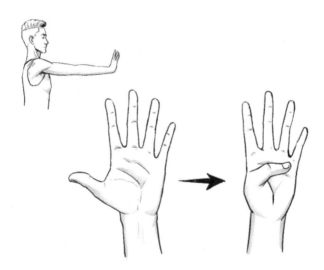

1. Place your arms out in front of you with your fingers stretched out. Your fingers should be pointing toward the ceiling.

2. Take your thumb and touch your pinky finger with it.

3. After you've touched your pinky with your thumb for a beat, you can return your thumb to the starting position.

4. Do this 10 times. This stretches your thumb, helping you to improve your grip strength.

Exercise 37. Wrist turn.

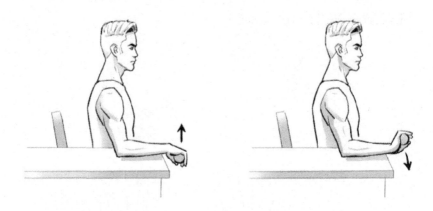

1. Get seated near a flat surface. Lay your forearm on this surface, but your hand and wrist should be hanging off the edge.

2. Hold an object that has some weight to challenge your wrist, but make sure that it's not too heavy, or it can put you at risk of hurting yourself.

3. Resist the weight as it drags your wrist down and then lift it up.

4. You can repeat this 10 times, but remember to be slow and steady.

5. Then practice the same thing with your other wrist.

Exercise 38. Clenched wrist turn.

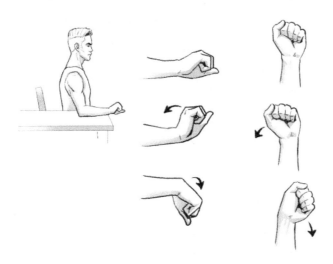

1. For this exercise, you will work both your wrist and your fingers. Be seated by a table for this exercise.
2. Clench your fist and hold your fingers tight. Place your forearm on the table at an angle, so that your hand is in the air and not resting on the table.
3. With your fists clenched, slowly move your wrist up and down without moving your arm. Do this 15 – 30 times.
4. Now move your clenched fists side to side using your wrist. Again do this 15 – 30 times.
5. This exercise helps to strengthen your wrists, while improving your grip strength.

Due to these exercises being easier and less strenuous on your body, you can practice them more frequently. They also won't take a lot of time in your day, so you can practice them every day when you're sitting and watching television or whenever you feel like it throughout the day. The more you practice these, the better your hand strength will be, which will not only help you perform your other exercises better, but also make your day-to-day life easier and less painful.

CORE STRENGTH

Let's take a look at some exercises that can improve your core strength. Improving your core strength as a senior is impera-tive, as it helps to increase your overall fitness, as well as providing you with more balance. As you age, your balance may become compromised, so having core strength will help you stay upright, and you won't fall as easily. Here are some exer-cises that will improve your core strength (Estrada, 2020):

Exercise 39. Plank.

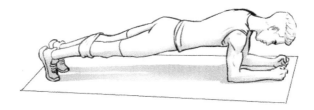

1. A popular core exercise that most of us have practiced at some point of our lives is the plank. It can be a very challenging exercise, especially with a resistance band added to it.

2. Place your resistance band around your calves, ensuring that the band has tension when your legs are hip-width apart.

3. Get into your plank position with your forearms flat on the ground and your toes supporting your lower half. Your elbows should be bent at a 90 degree angle and your shoulders should be staked directly over your elbows.

4. As you're in this plank position, ensure that your core muscles are engaged.

5. You can hold this plank for as long as you feel able, because it may be a more challenging and advanced exercise.

6. Try to challenge yourself by doing longer and longer planks with each core workout routine. For example, start by holding the plank position for 15 seconds and when that becomes easy try 30 seconds. Keep moving it up by 15 second intervals as you progress with your core exercises.

Exercise 40. Core side bends.

1. Stand in the middle of your resistance band with both feet at shoulder width apart. Your hands are at your sides with each end of the band in your hands. Keep your knees slightly bent. This is your starting position.

2. Bend your torso to the right while pulling your left elbow upward.

3. Return to the starting position and do the same with your left side. Bend your torso to the left while pulling up with your right elbow.

4. Return to the starting position. This completes one rep.

5. Do 10 – 20 reps and 2 – 3 sets on this exercise.

Exercise 41. Woodchopper.

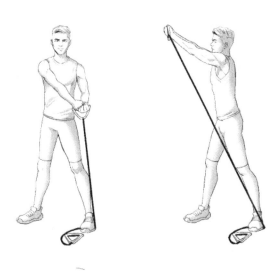

1. Start by stepping on top of one end of your resistance band with your left foot. Have the other end in both hands. Move your right foot out so your legs are a little wider than hip-width apart. Keep your arms straight and ensure the band has a little bit of give as you will be pulling it up across your body. Your arms should be

extended downwards towards your left foot. This is your starting position.

2. Lead with your hips and bring both arms up and across your chest in a diagonal line over your right shoulder.

3. With steady control bring your arms back down to the starting position. This will complete one rep.

4. Do 15 reps for 2 – 3 sets.

5. Now switch sides and perform the exercise for the same number of reps and set.

Exercise 42. Kneeling pallof press.

1. Anchor your resistance band somewhere stable and safe, ensuring that it's at chest level as you kneel on the floor.

2. Kneel on a mat or pillow for comfort, and hold onto the ends of your band with both hands.

3. Breathe in deeply, and then, as you exhale, straighten your arms as far away from your body as you can while still holding onto the resistance band.

4. Keep your core engaged as you hold this position for a few seconds.

5. As you inhale again, bring your arms and resistance band closer to your body.

6. While doing this exercise keep your knees hip-width apart, don't slouch forward or lean backwards. Also keep your shoulders level.

7. Do this 10 – 20 times, and 2 – 3 sets.

When we pursue a fitness journey, we can focus on upper body and lower body exercises, but forget about exercising our core. Although your core strength may be involved in some of these other exercises, taking time to work out your core specifically will only improve your overall fitness.

WARM-UPS AND COOL-DOWNS

Regardless of what types of exercises you're doing, their intensity, and how many exercises you do, you need to practice warm-ups and cool-downs. If you want to strengthen your muscles, you need to be able to prepare them for activity. Warm-ups help to activate and prepare your muscles for the exercises ahead, and cool-downs relieve the tension in your muscles so you avoid stiffness and pain the next day.

Warm-Up Exercises

There are various forms of warm-up exercises you can try. There may be a specific warm-up that you want to do for the certain exercise you're performing. You can try out various stretches and discover which ones warms you up the most, and allows you to have better performance throughout your exercise. These are some different forms of exercises you can look into.

- **Basic stretches.** These are stretches you've probably practiced before in your life, that you can now use as either a warm-up or cool-down.
- You can do a head tilt by moving your head to the side and using your hand to stretch it further.
- Then practice some shoulder circles by simply moving your shoulders in a circular motion.
- To warm up your arms, you can swing your arms back and forth.
- Marching on the spot is another way to stretch and warm up your entire body.
- **Dynamic stretches.** Doing dynamic stretches is one of the most popular ways for you to warm up. You want to avoid static stretches, which are short and fast stretches; dynamic stretches allow you to practice a full range of motion. Some dynamic stretches you can try include lunges and cycling.
- **Walking.** You may not think that walking is an effective warm-up, but it is, especially if you're doing a full-body workout. When you walk, you're moving your muscles and getting your blood flowing, which can prepare your muscles for an extensive workout. Another benefit of walking is weight loss. Walking for 30 minutes a day is great. But every minute you walk past that 30-minute mark you start to burn stored fat.

Whichever warm-up you choose to use, ensure you're doing it before each exercise. Find warm-up activities that get your blood flowing and your muscles stretched. Prioritizing warm-ups will allow you to have a productive workout.

Cool-Down Exercises

As much as warm-up exercises are important for you to perform your activities effectively, you must also engage in cool-down exercises after your workout so that you release the strain and tension in your muscles. This helps your muscles to recover at a faster rate. Here are some forms of cool-down activities you can try:

- **Yoga.** After an exercise, your body may be feeling tense, sore, and a little stressed. This makes yoga a great cool-down exercise method, as it is a form of activity that calms both your mind and body. End your workout with a few yoga poses to relieve tension in your muscles and relax your body. A few yoga positions you can do include the child's pose and reclining butterfly pose.
- **Stretches.** As with your warm-up exercises, stretches are a great form of activity to include in your cool-down routine. When you do your stretches, you should target the parts of your body that you exercised that day. For example, if you've exercised your upper body, you can do a standing forward bend. The above worm up stretches can also help cool you down from the intense exercise routine just completed.

- **Body shake.** As a senior beginning your fitness journey, you may be a bit out of shape. If you're starting off with some seated exercises, you can do some less intense cool-downs such as the body shake: Start by shaking out your arms and legs, then proceed to shake your whole body. Doing this for 30 seconds will help to relieve tension in your muscles, making you feel relaxed afterward.
- **Walking.** A great way to cool down after a workout is by walking. It keeps your body moving, allowing your heart rate to come down gradually and your muscles to cool down.

When you finish your workout routine, you may find yourself feeling very fatigued and tired, which makes it difficult for you to gather the energy to participate in cool-down exercises. You need to select specific cool-down activities that you find easier so that you can stick to them, even when you're tired after an intense workout. You should also make sure your warm-ups and cool-downs are targeting your core muscles.

CHOOSE EXERCISES THAT WORK BEST FOR YOU

It's valuable to try as many of these resistance band exercises as possible. Keep in mind the results you are working towards. You should start off by asking yourself what your goals are in terms of resistance strength training. Knowing this will help you to choose exercises that best target these muscles in your body.

If your personal goal is to increase the strength in your upper body, then you can practice some arm, shoulder, and torso resistance band exercises. Remember to introduce some variety to your routine so that you can holistically strengthen your body.

Once you determine which resistance band exercises are suitable for you, you should create a routine that utilizes all of these exercises. Having a suitable routine that targets all of your necessary muscles will provide you with the fitness growth you desire.

7

RESISTANCE ROUTINES

> *"You'll never change your life until you change some-thing you do daily. The secret of your success is found in your daily routine."*

— JOHN C. MAXWELL

The best way for you to develop resistance is through routine. You need to continuously introduce your body muscles to resistance training so that your body adapts to strength and resilience. Consistency is the key to training your muscles. If you aren't seeing the results and growth in your health and fitness that you desire, it may be due to lack of consistency.

If you create a healthy routine that both promotes consistency and allows time for you to relax and take care of your body, you will notice your body change in remarkable ways. Having a variety of routines that train the various muscles of your body helps you to spread out your exercises evenly. Sticking to your routines will ensure you'll improve your health and overall fitness.

TWO-WEEK PROGRAM

If you're getting started with your fitness journey, a 2-week program is a great way to start your routine. You can do a variety of exercises, as long as you're doing ones that are suitable for your fitness level, as well as targeting all parts of your body. These are just five different examples of exercise routines that you can experiment with, stick to, or use as inspiration to make your own program.

Routine 1: Seated Exercises

The first routine you can start off with features some seated exercises. If you haven't been exercising regularly and it's been a while since you've done any type of workout, then seated exercises are the best place to start. Seated exercises help your body to progressively work up to the more challenging workout routines.

Example seated exercise routine:

- Body shake for a few minutes.
- Practice 3 seated exercises discussed previously in this book, such as the row, chest press, and knee raises.
- Body shake for a few minutes.

Because your seated exercises are less intense and beginner-friendly, you don't have to do intense warm-ups or cool-downs. You can add as many seated exercises to your routine as you want, because they won't be strenuous on your body.

Routine 2: Core Strength

Your core strength can determine how fit and mobile you are. Once you get your muscles warmed up and used to exercise through your routine of seated exercises, you can move on to routines that focus on specific muscle groups. The first routine can target your core strength. If you have a stronger core, you will be able to improve your balance, mobility, and overall strength.

Core strength exercise routine:

- Warm up for 15 minutes. Refer back to the last chapter's section on Warm-Up Exercises for ideas!
- Practice 3 core exercises, such as the plank, core kick, and kneeling pallof press.
- Cool down for 5 minutes. Refer back to the last chapter's section on Cool-Down Exercises for ideas!

For all of these exercises, ensure that you're engaging your core.

Routine 3: Total-Body Workout

Focusing on specific muscle groups is valuable and effective, but you should also get into a routine where you work out your entire body. Strength resistance training is most beneficial when you're engaging all of your muscles at least one day in your week. For this routine, you can choose any exercises that you enjoy. All that matters is that you're picking a variety of exercises. You want to ensure that you're performing a full-body workout. That would include your upper body, core and lower body like legs and hips.

Total-body workout routine:

- Warm up for 15 minutes.
- Practice any 5 exercises throughout the book—for example, the head lift, lateral raise, leg press, hand clench, and plank.
- Cool down for 5 minutes.

This routine may be the most intense one, as you take the time and energy to engage each muscle in your body.

Routine 4: Upper Body

In the next routine, you can target your upper body. This means that you're engaging your shoulders, chest, arms, and upper back. The strength of your upper body is important as a senior.

Upper body routine:

- Warm up for 15 minutes.
- Practice 3 upper body exercises, such as lateral raises, tricep presses, and shoulder presses.

- Cool down for 5 minutes.

If fulfilling your daily tasks becomes more challenging for you, you need to prioritize some upper body workouts. Having enhanced strength in your upper body will allow you to lift, carry things, and move things with ease. Don't forget to add some grip strength and wrist strength activities to your upper body routine!

Routine 5: Lower Body

This routine helps you to focus on working out your lower body. This means you're doing exercises that engage your leg muscles, glutes, and calves. When you get older, walking around comfortably can be challenging, so doing these lower body exercises can strengthen your muscles and prepare you for more comfort as you walk.

Here is how to practice a lower body routine:

- Warm up for 15 minutes.
- Practice 3 lower body exercises, such as squats, lunges, and hip extensions.
- Cool down for 5 minutes.

When you focus on your lower body and strengthen your muscles, you will find that your mobility improves drastically. You're able to walk with more ease and practice your other exercises more effectively.

CHOOSING YOUR LEVELS

Once you've found a routine that works for you, and you know how you want to set out your schedule, you can choose different levels of intensity. You want to choose a level that is most suitable for you and your degree of fitness. Remember that you can try out all levels of intensity before committing to one. You won't know how fit you are until you try.

Absolute Beginners

Would you consider yourself an absolute beginner who hasn't exercised in a while? If so, this is the workout routine level you should explore. If you haven't exercised in a really long time, it's a safe option for you to start with the least intensive routine. You can progressively increase your levels once you feel the absolute beginner level becoming too easy for you. The beginner level entails the following:

- As an absolute beginner, you should only exercise 2 days a week, for 30 minutes per workout session.
- Your warm-up for each session should be 15 minutes.
- Routines 1, 4, and 5 are most optimal.
- Do 10 repetitions for each exercise, with 90 seconds of break in between.
- End with a cool-down.

This is a beginner's routine that can help you to get started. It may not seem like the most exercise, but it's a great starting point you'll build onto.

Beginner Intermediate

If the previous beginner's routine is too easy and simple for you, but you still don't feel fit enough to push yourself past your limits, you can try out the beginner intermediate level. This level will push you a little more, while still being easy on your body. Here's how to embrace the beginner intermediate exercise level:

- Exercise for 3 days in the week, for 30 minutes per workout session.
- Warm up for 15 minutes.
- Add Routines 1, 2, 4, and 5 to your workout.
- Practice each exercise 10 times, with a 90-second-long break in between.
- End with a 15-minute cool-down.

This level is similar to the previous one, but a few more exercises and workout elements will be added to your routine, which will help you to challenge yourself that little bit more.

Intermediate

If you're one of the more advanced seniors, who hasn't exercised in a short while but still has a degree of fitness, this is the routine for you! You go for walks frequently, as you have excellent mobility. These workouts may be a bit more intense, so if you need to take more breaks in between sets, you must do so! Here is how to go about practicing an intermediate routine:

- Exercise for 3 days a week, for 30 minutes per workout session.
- Warm up for 20 minutes.
- Add Routines 2, 3, 4, and 5 to your workout schedule.
- Practice each exercise 15 times, and have 90 seconds of rest in between sets.
- Cool yourself down with a low intense cool-down exercise. This should be for at least 10 minutes.

The intermediate level of exercise is quite similar to the beginner intermediate level. However, for this level, you repeat your exercises more, and focus on the more challenging workout routines.

Advanced

This workout routine is for you if you're very fit and capable of doing the more intense exercises. As a senior, it's suggested that you try other levels of intensity before jumping into advanced workouts. However, if you were exercising regularly prior to this, you can definitely start here. Let's take a look at what the advanced workout looks like:

- Exercise for 5 days of the week, at 30 minutes per session.
- Warm up for 20 minutes.
- Practice all routines and repeat them 30 times, with 90 seconds of rest between.
- Cool down for 10 minutes.

This advanced level means that you practice all of the workouts, instead of limiting yourself to a few routines. You must ensure you're exercising all of your muscles. You'll be repeating each exercise a lot more than the other levels.

Advanced Workout

If these five routines are a bit too simple for you, you can consider doing a more advanced workout that pushes you to your limits and gets your body moving. If you're looking to go the extra mile by pushing yourself with more advanced exercise, this workout is best for you. This resistance band advanced workout can take your fitness to the next level:

- Warm up for 15 minutes, and then perform:

  - 20 Banded shoulder presses.
  - 30 Banded lateral raises.
  - 30 Banded single arm rows on your left arm.
  - 30 Banded single arm rows on your right arm.
  - 30 Banded bicep curls.
  - 30 Back leg raises.
  - 30 Side leg raises.
  - 20 Squats.

- Repeat all of these banded exercises again.
- Plank for 2 to 5 minutes, or for as long as you can hold it.
- Cool down exercises for 10 minutes.

154 | ROBERT L. STONEBRIDGE

You may be thinking that this is a lot of exercise to accomplish in one workout session, but keep in mind that it is an advanced workout. Ensure you rest between each set, so you don't over-work yourself or feel too fatigued. You should only practice this exercise routine once a week—or maximum two times a week —along with your other exercises.

HOW TO SUPPORT YOUR NEW EXERCISE PROGRAM

Sticking to a routine can be challenging, especially when you feel tired and you're struggling to get started with your fitness journey. You may have a good day of exercise because you feel motivated, but as this motivation runs out, your routine becomes less consistent and you lose momentum.

This is a common problem that you're bound to be faced with during your health and fitness journey. Unfortunately, you can't rely on your motivation alone, as your motivation will run out eventually. This is why it's valuable to find efficient ways to support your new exercise program. You basically need to make it a habit. Something you just do daily. Like brushing your teeth or having dinner at a certain time every day, habits will take over when motivation fails. Here is how you can be supportive about your routine so that you can stay consistent and see real results:

- **Integrate it into your daily routine.** If you have a busy schedule or you just struggle to find the time or energy to bring exercise into your daily life, it's valuable to find ways to integrate it into your life. You need to make exercising a way of life for you so that you can feel energized and motivated to fulfill your exercise routine every day. If you go visit friends or family every day, you can find a way to integrate exercise to this schedule. For example, if they live close enough, you can walk to them.

- **Set goals.** A great way for you to stay on track is by setting manageable goals you work toward achieving on a daily basis. Goals that keep you accountable will help you to stick to a routine that brings you results. Ultimately, the right goals will lead you to success. Once a week, you should decide to set goals for each day that you then make an effort to achieve.

- **Reward yourself.** Being consistent with your exercises isn't always fun. There will be moments where you don't care about your fitness, and you feel too drained to keep going. In these moments, you should give yourself incentive to keep going! When we reward ourselves for being dedicated and consistent, it makes us want to push harder. For example, if you fulfill your two-week exercise program, you can reward yourself by going on an excursion that excites you, or eating your favorite food. We need to appreciate ourselves for looking after our health.

- **Develop other healthy habits.** If you're trying to live a healthier, fitter life, you should try to adapt to a healthier diet that motivates you to become fitter through consistent exercise programs. It could be most valuable for you to start your day off with a healthy habit. For example, you could drink sufficient water throughout the day or get enough sleep each night. When you start your day on a healthy note, it sets the tone for the rest of your day, which will ultimately motivate you to practice your new exercise routine.

- **Set habits and triggers.** A trigger is something that reminds you of something else. Like, if you hear the word peanut butter you might think of jelly as they normally go together. Have a trigger that reminds you to exercise. Like having your exercise cloths, shoes, and equipment out where it can be seen easily. Like on a coatrack or shelf by your front door. Next, set the exact time, place, and exercise you will be doing every day creating a habit for yourself. For example, at 1:00 pm every day I will do my exercise routine in my living room. Or, if you are doing walking that day. At 1:00 pm on Tuesday I will walk around the block 4 X. Habits can greatly improve your consistency in exercising on a regular basis.

It's important for you to make the effort to support yourself along this challenging journey. Your motivation may run out every now and then, so having a strong personal support system will keep you going. You need to hold yourself accountable and remain active even in the moments when you don't feel like being active and fit.

Finding What Works for You

Ultimately, you won't be able to support your fitness journey if you don't find a routine that works for you and makes you happy. You need to explore various exercises and determine which ones provide you with the most results, growth, and happiness. Once you curate a routine that you're satisfied with, you'll find yourself supporting it fully.

It's also important to switch up your routine every now and then, as you don't want to get yourself caught in a monotonous cycle. Trying out new routines will keep you on your toes, while still ensuring you're intrigued and excited to further your fitness journey. When you try out different routines, you're more likely to discover a routine that's perfect for you, which keeps you consistent.

MUSCLE RECOVERY

Wisdom is knowing when to have rest, when to have activity, and how much of each to have.

— SRI SRI RAVI SHANKAR

No matter how fit you are, you need to rest your muscles. You won't be able to be productive with your exercises if you don't give your muscles time to recover. Taking the necessary time to rest, sleep, and take days off will only improve your results in your fitness journey. You will find that you're a lot fitter, more flexible, and more capable than you ever thought you were when you recover those muscles and continue working on your fitness consistently.

WHY YOU NEED REST DAYS

Throughout this book we've emphasized how important it is to stay consistent with your exercises. Although this is true, you need to take time to rest to achieve muscle recovery. If your muscles don't get the time to rest, it will reflect in your performance. If you're an ambitious person you may want to keep pushing yourself, but rest days help with:

- **Alleviating muscle pain.** This is the most common reason why people take rest days. Exercising regularly and pushing yourself to your limits is bound to leave you with a few aches and pains. The best way for you to prevent this from happening is by taking those rest days to allow your body to rejuvenate and feel better.
- **Repairing and building muscle.** If you want to build muscle, you may be thinking that the more you push yourself, the better. Although consistency and effort are crucial for muscle development, no muscles will grow if you don't give them time to repair themselves. Rest days provide your muscles with the opportunity to restore those muscles so that they can be built more later.
- **Replenishing your body's energy.** You won't be able to perform your exercises to the best of your ability when your body is drained. Being burnt out physically means that your body becomes more fatigued. You can't do as many exercises as before, and when you try to, you don't perform them with efficiency and accuracy. When you take those necessary rest days, you replenish your

energy, making it easier for you to be productive when you begin to exercise again.

None of us like to admit that we have our moments of weakness. You may want to be strong, fit, and capable of exercising every day without needing a break, but this is neither realistic nor healthy for you. No mater your age, whether young or old, resting and letting your muscles heal and grew is essential for everyone.

HOW MANY REST DAYS SENIORS NEED

A question you may be asking yourself is whether you require more rest days because of your age. As a senior, your body isn't as fit, agile, and tolerant as it used to be. Doing exercises may be more challenging, but the benefits you will experience will be rewarding. If you want to make the most of your fitness journey without finding yourself burnt out, fatigued, or injured, you must get sufficient rest days.

It's crucial for every individual who is frequently active to have their rest days. Seniors need to be more mindful of taking rest days, as neglecting them can be catastrophic. This is how you can determine the number of rest days you need as a senior:

- **Exercise every other day.** As a senior, you don't require intense workouts every single day in order to get fitter. Exercising every day will only hurt you in the long run. You can exercise every other day and experience the results that you desire. If you're keeping active for at least 30 minutes every other day, you will reap the benefits of a fit and healthy lifestyle.

- **Consider how intense your exercise routine is.** If you're doing more intense workouts on your active days, you must have more rest days so that you can recover. If your workout routines are more casual and less intense, you can have fewer rest days. The more you exert your muscles, the more time you'll need to recover and replenish your strength.

- **Schedule your rest days.** If you want a definite answer of how many rest days you require, a nice standard amount active people use is 5 days active and 2 days rest. Whatever amount of rest days you choose, you need to learn how to spread them out evenly. If you choose to have 3 rest days, you can have 2 active days, a rest day, another 2 active days, and then a rest day. Ensure you schedule your rest days evenly.

SIGNS YOU NEED A REST DAY

Although we've established that seniors must prioritize rest, the answer to this question is subjective for each individual. You should have as many rest days as your body requires, even if you find yourself having more rest days in a week than active days. Listening to your body is key!

When you get into the swing of working out, you may get so involved that you exercise every day. Because you get so caught up in this routine, you never take time to relax or have rest days. When you start your fitness journey, you need to start understanding your body, so you know when it's time to rest and recover. A great way for you to learn this is by identifying the signs of needing a rest day.

Feeling Burnt Out

One of the main signs of needing a rest day is feeling burnt out. If you're starting to feel burnt out both physically and mentally, it's time for you to rest. It will get in the way of your productivity, as you aren't able to give it your all through your exercises. But what does it *feel* like to be burnt out? These are some signs and symptoms are being burnt out:

- **Fatigue.** The main and most noticeable sign of burnout is being fatigued. As a senior you may find that you're more tired than usual, but if you're experiencing more fatigue than you're used to, it's a sign that your body needs a rest. Pushing your body can be a very draining experience.
- **Difficulty concentrating.** If you feel as though your concentration levels are decreasing, this may be a sign that you're burnt out. Exercising a lot doesn't only take a toll on you physically: It can also impact you mentally. When your body is feeling drained, it causes you to mentally struggle as well.
- **Anxiety.** Are you feeling more anxious and stressed than you usually do? Being exhausted can cause you to feel more on edge, as you don't have the energy to deal with stressful situations. When you're more fatigued, it's more challenging to deal with everyday stress.

- **Sluggishness after your workout.** It's normal to feel physically tired after your workout. Your body is tired, sweaty, and maybe a little sore. However, an hour or two after your workout, you should feel a boost in your energy. If you're feeling sluggish for the rest of the day and unable to perform your daily tasks, you should use the following day for rest.

Ultimately, you want to use exercise to make yourself feel stronger and happier, so you can live longer. If you are working out excessively to the point where it negatively impacts your day-to-day life, you need to make more of an effort to prioritize rest days.

Sore Body

If your body is starting to feel really sore, you probably need to give it a break. It's normal to have a few muscle aches and pains, especially if you haven't been doing much exercise prior. When your body feels too stiff and sore as you're trying to move around and do exercises, you need to rest so it recovers.

The more you push yourself with these exercises, the more aches and pains you will experience. As a senior, you can perform more activities than people may realize, but being older can make you subject to more unwanted aches and pains. This shouldn't discourage you on your journey, as it should just be a reminder to you that you need to rest and recover.

It's important to keep note of what types of pains you're feeling. If you're having beginner's pains because you pushed your body to it's limit during your exercises, then you shouldn't worry. Beginner's pain is focused on your muscles, as you may feel sore or achy, and this usually lasts only a day or two in the targeted areas you've exercised. However, if you're having consistent pain after exercises, pain that provides you with a lot of lasting discomfort, you should consider going to seek professional care and advice.

You may find out that you have bad back problems because, every time you exercise, your back feels really painful. If this is the case, you will need a doctor or professional to inform you of what exercises you can and can't do, to ensure your back is not injured further. Keep track of the different aches and pains in your body so you know what's serious and what's nothing to worry about.

Easily Getting Injured or Falling Ill

When you push your body too hard, you not only experience more muscle pain and achiness, but you also risk getting yourself injured. When your muscles, tendons, and ligaments are more fatigued and strained, you're more likely to get hurt when you're exercising.

We've established that exercising too intensely can cause you to burn out, which causes fatigue. When you're exhausted, your immune system isn't as strong. This causes you to catch illnesses more easily. If you find yourself getting a cold or flu more frequently than you're used to, it could be a sign that you're pushing yourself too much.

Inability to Finish a Workout Routine

If you find yourself struggling to get through a workout routine that you usually find easy, you're probably in need of some rest. Because you've been consistently exercising so much, you don't have the energy you may have had in the beginning of the week. As you're doing your workout routine, you find yourself out of breath and in pain.

When you experience an exercise session like this, where your body feels like it's not cooperating, don't force it. You may want to push through it so that you can be proud of your consistency, but pushing yourself past your limits will only hurt you in the long run. The best thing to do is stop your exercise, rest, and try again the next day.

ACTIVE REST DAYS

You want to have a rest day because you're feeling drained, but you still want to stay consistent and active. There are some less intensive activities you can do that allow your muscles to relax while still getting your body moving. You may find that having these active rest days helps you to achieve your goals faster. It also prevents you from falling out of your consistent routine. Here are some ways you can spend your active rest days:

- **Stretching.** If your muscles are feeling sore from all of the resistance training you've been doing, effective stretching exercises will help. A large part of muscle recovery is all about stretching. This will help to relieve any pain or stiffness you have. When you spend your rest days stretching, you prepare your body to do more exercises the next day.

- **Walking.** An amazing form of exercise that can be a lot less intensive is walking. Walking can actually be a form of stretching that will help to both warm up and cool down your muscles. Spending your rest days walking can provide you with various benefits, as it's great for your mental health, quality of life, weight, and productivity towards your other exercises. You can go for low-intensity strolls and still experience benefits from it on your rest days.

- **Playing a sport.** But, if you're playing a sport on your rest day, ensure that you aren't overdoing it. Many sports require a lot of strength and energy. If you're practicing strength training intensely and spending all of your rest days playing sports, you won't give your muscles enough time to recover.

- **Practicing a hobby.** Your rest day is the perfect opportunity for you to practice your hobby, which may be something controlled, seated, in your home—or it could be something more active. Maybe one of your favorite hobbies is to garden. Gardening requires a certain level of activity as you pull out weeds, dig, bend over to plant, and move around a lot. It's an enjoyable, yet active way to spend your rest day.

- **Socializing.** Maybe you want to spend your rest day with friends, family, or strangers who want to build new relationships. Going out and doing fun activities can be a great way to spend your active rest day. You could just go to the park or the beach and enjoy your day off of your exercise routine. You can also practice other active rest day activities with your loved ones, such as walking and practicing hobbies.

These are all low-intensity activities that don't have to necessarily be exercise. You may just want to do these activities for fun. Although it's great to have your active rest days, it's also important to have those lazy rest days where you do nothing. You should wake up late, watch movies all day, read a good book, or take as many naps as your body needs. We all deserve those off days where we do absolutely nothing. You will find that it's nourishing for both your mind and body!

MASSAGE YOUR MUSCLES

If you've done your stretches, warm-ups, and cool-downs, but your body muscles still feel sore, you should try muscle massages. Having a massage can be an extremely soothing way to relieve any pain or stiffness you have. People often view massages as a luxury spa treatment, but you'd be surprised to find out how effective massages could be for you.

Benefits of Massages

As we've stated, massages are beneficial for you to decrease pain in your muscles and joints. Massages can also be beneficial for other reasons. They are soothing acts that can make us feel good holistically. These are some benefits you can experience from massaging your muscles:

- **Reducing stress.** Massages can act as a relaxant. If your body is feeling tense from being stressed, then massaging your muscles can help you to relax them. Feeling more relaxed physically can have a positive impact on you mentally. Massages can even go as far as reducing your anxiety. Struggling with anxiety can take a large toll on your body. For example, you may have insomnia, which prevents you from sleeping at night. Getting regular massages will promote healthy sleep, while mitigating your insomnia.

- **Relieving pain from minor injuries.** If you push yourself too hard and experience an injury, a massage could be exactly what you need to relieve this pain. Not only will it help decrease the pain you're experiencing, but it will cause your injury to heal at a faster rate. The quicker you're able to heal from an injury, the better, so that you can continue with your fitness routine. It's important to know whether it's a major or minor injury. If you're experiencing a major injury, a massage may make you feel worse and cause further damage, unless you consult a doctor and they give you specific instructions. But, if it's a minor injury like sore biceps, a massage is exactly what you need!

- **Boosting your energy.** As a senior, you may find that exercising regularly leaves you feeling drained and fatigued. You want to be consistent with your routines, but when you try to exercise, your muscles feel too tired to keep going. Getting massages improves your blood circulation, which results in a boost of energy. When your blood circulation improves, it provides your body with more oxygen.

- **Improving your health.** Massages aren't only valuable for your body's fitness: They can also improve other aspects of your physical health. Getting massaged around your abdominal area can improve your gut health, as it stimulates peristalsis. Peristalsis is the act of your intestines relaxing and contracting, which stimulates the movement of your stool throughout your digestive system, until you're able to excrete it. As stated before, massages can help relieve any existing pain in your joints or back that you may be experiencing from old age. They can also boost your immune system and reduce headaches.

There are no negatives you can experience from getting a good, professional massage. You may think that massages are a luxury you don't necessarily need, but once you start receiving them, you'll notice how beneficial they become for your fitness journey, as well as your overall health and happiness. Your performance for the resistance band strength training will be better than ever before.

Types of Massages

There are various types of massages you can try to help your muscles recover and grow. These different types of massages can be used for various purposes. You can determine which massage is suitable for you and your needs. Here are a few forms of massages that you can look into:

- **Swedish massage.** This massage is gentle and is used to relax your muscles, improve blood circulation, and energize you. This massage has a combination of long, kneading strokes and short strokes. It releases tension in your body, as the masseuse applies light to medium pressure through their strokes.

- **Sports massage.** You may think that this form of massage is for athletes, but it is suitable for any person who has experienced injury through physical activity, or for individuals trying to decrease and ease muscle pain. This massage requires faster strokes than the traditional Swedish massage. It aims to target specific muscle groups.

- **Deep massage.** If you're looking for deeper, more effective results, the deep-tissue massage is something you should look into. This massage requires more intense strokes, as your massage therapist will apply more pressure to relieve tension and knots in your muscles. Although it's a more intense massage, it should not be painful or too uncomfortable.

- **Trigger point massage.** This massage is aimed to treat specific spots in your muscles and joints. It relieves tension in your muscles by increasing the temperature and blood flow, which influences relaxation. When your muscles are relaxed, they're able to become restored more rapidly. It also increases your flexibility when you exercise.

Depending on what your need for a massage is, which muscles you're trying to target, and where you're feeling pain, you can decide which massage is suitable for you. You may want to try out all these types of massages, to see which one works best for you. If you're visiting a professional for this service, they can inform you on different types of massages your body may require.

Where and How to Get a Massage

If you're looking to get a more serious type of massage like a deep tissue, trigger point, or sports massage, you should seek help from a professional. These more intense massages can't be performed by just anyone, because you could risk further injury.

There are various massage professionals out there who can target your different muscles. When you look for someone, you should ensure that they are licensed and have the training and experience you need. Determine how many visits you'll need from them, and find out whether it can be covered by your medical insurance.

If you don't want to do formal and professional massages, you can look into doing them at home. For more gentle massages, like the Swedish massage, you can get a close friend or family member to do them for you. You can even perform these gentle massages on yourself. All you need to do is rub the muscles that feel a bit sore after you've worked them.

Another way for you to achieve an at home massage is by using foam rollers. These are cylindrical objects that can be placed under your targeted muscles. For example, if you want to massage your leg muscles, you can place the foam roller underneath your legs and roll them over it. This helps to relieve the pain in your muscles.

CREATING YOUR OWN REST DAY ROUTINE

After reading the benefits of and needs for having rest days in your routine, it's time for you to incorporate rest days into your fitness schedule. As stated earlier, it's valuable for you to plan your exercise routine ahead of time. If you don't plan rest days ahead of time, you may end up neglecting them. This will cause you to exercise until you burn out. Taking regular rest days will keep you on track to your fitness goals, as you're able to exercise consistently at peak performance.

Another way for you to motivate yourself and ensure you're taking the rest days you require is by planning what to do on each rest day. You can plan fun, active rest days where you're doing what makes you happy; or you could plan to do absolutely nothing, to let your body rest completely. Knowing what you'll be doing on your rest days gives you something to look forward to.

CONCLUSION

 Take care of your body, it's the only place you have to live.

— JIM ROHN

We are only given one body in our lifetime, and it's up to us to know how to look after it properly so that we live a long and healthy life. Many of us take our bodies for granted, especially when we're younger, because we feel invincible. When we don't take care of our bodies when we're younger, we start to feel the repercussions when we're older.

Just because you're experiencing aches and pains, you're out of shape, and you have compromised mobility doesn't mean you can't recover your strength and fitness as a senior. There's a common misconception that the elderly have an inability to exercise and truly push themselves. This couldn't be further from the truth, because with consistency, healthy habits, and patience, you will acquire the strength and level of fitness you desire.

Although you mustn't limit yourself as a senior, it's also important for you to seek professional advice before you get onto a workout program or routine. Your body isn't as agile as it used to be, and you may have health conditions that could end up compromising your workout. After seeing a doctor or physical therapist, you will know your body's limitations, as well as discover how to push yourself safely.

If you're seeking consistency and growth, you should look into creating a routine that works best for you. Everyone's body is different, so you need to find your own exercises that are more suitable for your body, possible conditions, and level of fitness. Try out all of the resistance band exercises throughout this book and put together a routine that targets all the right muscles.

The key to success in exercise is taking it on a gradient. Set a goal of what you want to accomplish and set up habits to get you there. You can get physically fit and live a live a fantastic life! These are some success stories that will motivate you to persevere through your journey.

Barry's daughter wanted to ensure that her father maintained his health so that his independence and quality of life wouldn't degrade as he aged. This is why she motivated him to start his fitness journey. With determination and hard work, Barry became fitter than many young teens. He was able to hold a plank for 2 minutes and 30 seconds and fulfill complex training courses. This has allowed him to keep his independence, improve his mobility, and even increase his bone density!

81-year-old Gordon has been practicing strength training for 50 years of his life, which has allowed him to live the long and healthy life he's enjoying. Instead of quitting his training due to old age, he completed his aging process with strength training. He stated that his dedication to strength training not only kept him healthy and strong, but also contributed to his mental health. Although he's in his 80s, he's still mentally sharp and confident, which is due to his hard work.

These positive success stories should inspire you. This book has provided you with all of the tools you need to get started on your fitness journey as a senior. I hope you enjoyed it, and please leave a review, letting us know what you think. Happy exercising!

service@yellowworkoutbook.com

REFERENCES

Bailey, A. (2010, April 20). *Resistance band exercises for seniors.* LIVESTRONG.COM; Livestrong.com. https://www.livestrong.com/article/108869-resistance-band-exercises-seniors/

Barrosos, M. (2020, October 2). *How long should you rest between sets?* Bodybuilding.com. https://www.bodybuilding.com/content/how-long-should-you-rest-between-sets.html

Beaumont. (n.d.). *Cardiovascular training Vs. Strength training | Beaumont Weight Loss | Beaumont Health.* Www.beaumont.org. https://www.beaumont.org/services/weight-loss/cardiovascular-training-vs-strength-training-for-weight-loss

Bugden, K. (2020, September 20). *10 Best resistance band exercises for seniors.* Athletic Muscle. https://athleticmuscle.com/resistance-band-exercises-for-seniors/

Cleveland Clinic. (2019, October 25). *Should you try resistance bands for strength training?* Health Essentials from Cleveland Clinic. https://health.clevelandclinic.org/should-you-try-resistance-bands-for-strength-training/

Coila, B. (2018, December 27). *Effects of nutrition & exercise on muscle & bone health.* Healthy Eating | SF Gate. https://healthyeating.sfgate.com/effects-nutrition-exercise-muscle-bone-health-3526.html

Davis, N. (2018, September 18). *How to inhale and exhale your way to better, stronger fitness.* Healthline. https://www.healthline.com/health/fitness-exercise/when-to-inhale-and-exhale-during-exercise

Estrada, J. (2020, September 6). *9 Resistance bands exercises perfect for beginners.* Well+Good. https://www.wellandgood.com/resistance-bands-exercises-beginners/

Finlay, L. (2022, October 24). *Here's how to choose the right resistance bands and how to use them.* Verywell Fit. https://www.verywellfit.com/choosing-and-using-resistance-bands-1229709

Fit, J. (2021, January 3). *4 Easy neck strengthening exercises to increase mobility.* Doc Jen Fit | Doctor of Physical Therapy. https://www.docjenfit.com/neck-strengthening-exercises/

Fletcher, J. (2021, January 28). *Rest days: Why they are important, benefits, and when to take one.* Www.medicalnewstoday.com. https://www.medicalnew stoday.com/articles/rest-day

Fontaine, D. (2021, May 18). *Geriatric massage: Benefits, considerations, cost & more.* Healthline. https://www.healthline.com/health/geriatric-massage

Freya. (2020, August 13). *17 Inspirational quotes about choices in life [with printable designs].* Www.happierwithtea.com. https://www.happierwithtea.com/quotes-about-choices-in-life/

Green, D. A. (n.d.). *Wrist and hand rehab part I.* Back Pain and Headache Specialist - Burke va - NOVA Headache & Chiropractic Center. Retrieved January 23, 2023, from https://www.novaheadache.com/blog/chiropractic-burke-hand-rehab-chiropractor

Harvard Health Publishing. (2021, October 13). *Strength training builds more than muscles - Harvard Health.* Harvard Health; Harvard Health. https://www.health.harvard.edu/staying-healthy/strength-training-builds-more-than-muscles

Holly, A. (2021a, July 13). *65 Positive aging quotes about getting older gracefully.* Quoteflick.com. https://quoteflick.com/quotes-about-aging-gracefully/

Holly, A. (2021b, July 14). *80 of the best one liners about life to make you smile.* Quoteflick.com. https://quoteflick.com/one-liners-about-life/

Julom, M. (2022, July 26). *The Ultimate 8 week resistance band training program (with PDF).* This Is Why I'm Fit. https://www.thisiswhyimfit.com/resistance-band-workout-routine/

Kerr, C. (2021, April 25). *Top 50 motivational workout quotes.* Upper Hand. https://upperhand.com/50-motivational-workout-quotes/

MacPherson, R. (2021, July 14). *How effective are resistance bands?* Verywell Fit. https://www.verywellfit.com/are-resistance-bands-effective-5191733

Mayer, F., Scharhag-Rosenberger, F., Carlsohn, A., Cassel, M., Müller, S., & Scharhag, J. (2011). The intensity and effects of strength training in the elderly. *Deutsches Ärzteblatt Online 108(21).* https://doi.org/10.3238/arztebl.2011.0359

McCracken, M. (2017, April 10). *This is how many rest days experts say you need per week.* Brit + Co. https://www.brit.co/how-many-rest-days-per-week/

MedlinePlus. (2019). *Nutrition for older adults.* Medlineplus.gov; National Library of Medicine. https://medlineplus.gov/nutritionforolderadults.html

Migala, J. (2022, April 13). *How to use resistance bands: For absolute beginners.* EverydayHealth.com. https://www.everydayhealth.com/fitness/how-to-get-started-with-resistance-band-workouts-an-absolute-beginners-guide/

Mike. (2018, May 3). *Key nutrients necessary for healthy bones and muscle.* London Osteoporosis Clinic. https://www.londonosteoporosisclinic.com/key-nutritents-necessary-for-healthy-bones-and-muscle/

Mike. (2021, December 26). *Full body resistance band loop workout for seniors and beginners | All Seated | 25Min.* Senior Fitness with Meredith. https://www.seniorfitnesswithmeredith.com/full-body-resistance-band-loop-workout-for-seniors-and-beginners-all-seated-25min/

National Institute on Aging. (n.d.). *10 Myths about aging.* National Institute on Aging. https://www.nia.nih.gov/health/10-myths-about-aging

NCOA. (2021, August 23). *The national council on aging.* Www.ncoa.org. https://www.ncoa.org/article/how-to-stay-hydrated-for-better-health

NHS. (2020, April 30). *Warm-up and cool-down.* Www.nhsinform.scot. https://www.nhsinform.scot/healthy-living/keeping-active/before-and-after-exercise/warm-up-and-cool-down

NHS 24. (2019). *Exercises for wrist, hand and finger problems.* Nhsinform.scot. https://www.nhsinform.scot/illnesses-and-conditions/muscle-bone-and-joints/exercises/exercises-for-wrist-hand-and-finger-problems

Pelzer, K. (2021, September 24). *Take a deep breath in, now release, and find inner peace with these 100 yoga quotes!* Parade: Entertainment, Recipes, Health, Life, Holidays. https://parade.com/1158471/kelseypelzer/yoga-quotes/

ProsourceFit. (2017, August 15). *9 Reasons to use resistance bands for working out.* ProsourceFit. https://www.prosourcefit.com/blogs/news/9-reasons-to-use-resistance-bands-for-working-out

Selig, M. (2018, November 4). *6 ways to discover and choose your core values.* Psychology Today. https://www.psychologytoday.com/us/blog/change-power/201811/6-ways-discover-and-choose-your-core-values

Sorenson, M. (2021, March 25). *Senior citizens obtain vitamin D from sunshine.* Sunlight Institute. https://sunlightinstitute.org/senior-citizens-vitamin-d-cutaneous-sun-exposure/

The #1 reason you need consistent exercise. (2018, June 12). OSR Physical Therapy. https://www.osrpt.com/2018/06/reason-you-need-consistent-exercise/

Theifels, J. (2017, April 21). *How to breathe while working out, exercising.* AARP. https://www.aarp.org/health/healthy-living/info-2017/breathe-exercise-workout.html

Third Age Fitness. (n.d.). *8 Standing resistance band exercises for older adults and seniors to build lower body strength*. Third Age Fitness. Retrieved January 23, 2023, from https://www.thirdagefitness.com.au/pages/8-standing-resistance-band-exercises-for-older-adults-and-seniors-to-build-lower-body-strength

Tri-City Medical Center. (n.d.). *Why Warming Up and Cooling Down is Important*. https://www.tricitymed.org/2016/12/warming-cooling-important/#:

Tweed, K. (2014, June 30). *6 Myths about exercise and aging*. WebMD; WebMD. https://www.webmd.com/fitness-exercise/guide/exercise-and-aging-myths

USA, H. (2019, October 8). *The truth about exercise after 70*. HUR USA - for LIFELONG STRENGTH. https://www.hurusa.com/the-truth-about-exercise-after-70/

Volpi, E., Nazemi, R., & Fujita, S. (2004). Muscle tissue changes with aging. *Current Opinion in Clinical Nutrition and Metabolic Care, 7*(4), 405–410. https://doi.org/10.1097/01.mco.0000134362.76653.b2

Williamson, J. (2019, March 14). *14 Quotes about rest & being kind enough to give yourself a break*. Healing Brave. https://healingbrave.com/blogs/all/quotes-about-rest-give-yourself-a-break

45 Best Habit Quote Collection To Inspire You | Evolve (evolveinc.io)

Made in the USA
Las Vegas, NV
03 December 2024

13183120R00105